The FUTURE of CLEAN ENERGY

Who Wins and Who Loses as the World Goes Green

GARY SCHWENDIMAN

authorHOUSE®

AuthorHouse™
1663 Liberty Drive
Bloomington, IN 47403
www.authorhouse.com
Phone: 1 (800) 839-8640

Published by AuthorHouse 03/18/2016

ISBN: 978-1-4969-4043-8 (sc)
ISBN: 978-1-4969-4042-1 (hc)
ISBN: 978-1-4969-4041-4 (e)

Library of Congress Control Number: 2014916581

Print information available on the last page.

To my family:

My father and mother, John and Naomi; my brothers and sister, Leo, Carl, Dee, Gene, and Karen; my children, Todd, Heidi, Lisa, Wendy, and Julie; their spouses, Suzanne, Jon, Scott, Matt, and Sterling; and my grandchildren, Katrina, Cameron, Sarah, Hannah, Madison, Megan, Molly, Annie, Lincoln, Whitney, Justin, Quincy, Simon, and Garrison.

Contents

Acknowledgements

The people whose influence, inspiration, support, and friendship have contributed to the writing of this book and in my career as an educator, university professor, dean, and now private equity executive are far too many to mention. I will inevitably fail to acknowledge many of them. To all who have helped me along the way, you know who you are, and I thank you.

While some have said that age, experience, and compound interest will always defeat skill and youth, I have to say that the hundreds of students and graduate students with whom I have worked in research over the years would be superbly competitive in any contest. I offer my abundant thanks to the two brilliant research assistants whose work was so instrumental in the completion of this book. Mark Sidorenkov and his monumental research skills were the engines that drove the first draft. Josh DiBiasi, another exceptional researcher, stepped to the plate for the second and final drafts and knocked it out of the park.

My deepest thanks to my editor and writing advisor Kyle Fager, my marketing and graphic design specialist Mandy Stoffel, and my senior research assistant Ela Harrison. Without these three brilliant people, this book never would have made it to its compelling completion or found its way into your hands.

I must also thank the many professors and other scholars from whom I learned to think in conceptual frameworks. Those frameworks served as the foundation of my interest in many areas of knowledge, including clean energy. So to Professor H. G. Wells (no, not *that* H. G. Wells, but an excellent professor at Washington State University by the same name), I thank you for helping me to first turn on my academic lights. From the time of Professor Wells's philosophy class right up until I achieved my PhD, I found the world of science opened up and filled by great professors like Chris Anderson, Les Cooper, Phil Daniels, William Dyer, Kenneth Hardy, Larry Jensen, Daryl Pedersen, and David Stimpson.

To my professorial colleagues at the General Motors Institute, especially Tony Hain, Gary Richetto, and Stewart Tubbs, thank you for working with me to teach management skills and conduct research on the automotive industry. One of my colleagues, Ron Smith, left General Motors to become dean of the College of Business Administration at the University of Nebraska. Though I was only 33 years old at the time, he invited me to join him at Nebraska as assistant dean. Four years later, Ron left to become a dean of the business school at Georgetown University, and I took the mantle as dean at Nebraska, where I served for 17 years.

The professorial colleagues and students who inspired me to be a better professor and dean at the University of Nebraska are many. I learned from them all. To the thousands of students to whom I handed out graduation diplomas over 17 years, thank you for making me proud to be your dean. Thank you also to the presidents and chancellors of the University of Nebraska with whom I served: Martin Massengale, Ron Roskens, and Steve Sample. Thank you to my fellow deans Max Larsen, Stan Liberty, Gerald Meisels, Harvey Perlman, Bob Simerly, Cecil Steward, and John Strong; associate deans Gordon Karels, Art Kraft, Ron Hampton, Clay Singleton, Nancy Stara, and D'vee Buss; department chairs Jack Goebel, Sanford Grossbart, Tom Hubbard, Charles Lamphear, Sang Lee, Craig MacPhee, and Manfred Peterson; and professors John Anderson, Tom Balke, John Brasch, Kung Chen, Richard DeFusco, Les Digman, Fred Luthans, Campbell McConnell, Bob Mittelstaedt, Jerry Petr, Colin Ramsey, George Rejda, Jim Schmidt, Marc Schneiderjans, Bill Walstad, and Tom Zorn. My thanks to Professor Martin Holmes and Professor Nick Horsewood of Oxford University, who added an international dimension of knowledge to my thought processes while I was in Oxford with Nebraska students over parts of six summers.

Finally, thank you to the business leaders and others who have been inspirational to me and supportive of me over the years: Jim Abel, Duane Acklie, Harold Andersen, Richard Bank, Scott Brittenham, Jeff Broin, Clyde Boutelle, Warren Buffett, Tom Buis, Terry Busch, Bob Campos, Wesley Clark, Jim Clifton, Mike Cox, Don Dillon, Bob Dineen, Roy Dinsdale, Alice Dittman, Ron Fagen, Bill Fairfield, Terry Fairfield, Grant Gregory,

Vinod Gupta, Mike Harper, Ron Harris, Bob Harris, Jonathan Henness, Tom Henning, Skip Hove, Marlin Jensen, Alan Keele, Marc LeBaron, Carl Mammel, Tim Manring, Mickey Mays, Chuck Miller, Michael Ning, Terry Pierson, Jack Porter, Gary Riggs, Andrew Schwendiman, Carl Schwendiman, Gene Schwendiman, Todd Schwendiman, Clay Smith, Jan Thayer, Dale Tintsman, Don Tomlinson, Chuck Torrey, Robert Valentine, and Dave Vander Griend.

Introduction

All my life I've been a teacher. I've taught students as a professor and dean at the University of Nebraska, and I've taught executives at the General Motors Institute and other corporations across the nation. Over the course of those many years, I discovered that a particular strength of mine is that I'm able to take complicated theoretical concepts and explain them in practical and compelling ways that people can easily understand. That's what I've tried to do in this book.

Before we apply that effort to the future of clean energy, I must alert you to two things. First, I intend to present this book in a fun and engaging way. Second, at no point should you think of this as a book designed to provide an analytical, textbook-style study on clean energy. Yes, you'll find data points and endnotes throughout, but I offer those merely as a way to provide context for the ultimate goal. What is the ultimate goal? To show you a framework for understanding and evaluating clean energy in the future. All those exhaustive studies of global warming, economics, the environment, and energy policy I'll leave to other authors and other books.

That said, I'm also not going to give you the elementary guide to energy production and consumption. The scope of this book lies somewhere between. We won't be data mining, nor will we be taking a blanket look at what clean energy is without offering some structures and solutions for overcoming the world's present and future economic and environmental problems. Mostly, we're just going to have fun learning the basics about the trends I've observed in American electricity and global fuel consumption. Then we can see if those trends lead us to some conclusions about how the future of clean energy might look.

I've always believed that the best explanation is the one that's easiest to understand. If we can boil complicated concepts down to their essence, it leads to greater understanding and education than you would expect otherwise. For example, when Warren Buffett's partner, Charlie Munger, was asked how he and Warren had created such an investment empire, he didn't tell his audience to "read this book" or "follow these twenty principles." He said instead, "We're rational."[1] So the totality of the success of the greatest investors who have ever lived can be explained in two words. I've tried to create this examination of clean energy in a way that's similarly easy to understand, without skimping on the important stuff.

So if you're looking for the be-all and end-all of clean energy statistics, I invite you to enjoy this book for what it is, and I direct you to the many websites and books presenting the data that led to my conclusions. In these pages, you'll find only the major concepts. The myriad offshoots, debates, and academic investigations they may spark? Well, you can pursue them via the works cited. You will find those works in the endnotes at the back of the book. If you're the type who likes to discover things for yourself, I think you will enjoy the way these source materials further enhance your knowledge on the future of clean energy.

I'm going to make many bold statements in the coming pages, but let me start with one that's not so bold: global society is experiencing major information overload. With all the media we can and do consume, we're forced to process more information in any given day than anyone who ever lived before us. That's a pretty astounding thought, but it's absolutely true. So what do we do with this tremendous fog of information? How do we pick through all the junk to learn something important?

It starts with a framework. Information is only useful and memorable in the context of a greater whole that is easy to understand. We're about to start discussing some big topics here—electricity production and use; oil, gasoline, natural gas, and ethanol; the future of the automobile engine; global agriculture; nuclear power; global warming; and of course, how all these things interact with one another. How in the world could I possibly impart all that information to you without a framework on which to hang it?

The answer is that I couldn't. So I've created a framework that I believe will make these otherwise complicated topics and their relationships to one another easier to understand. Now, I recognize that not everyone follows

American football, but most people have at least a passing awareness of the sport. With this in mind, I chose to analyze each energy source as if it were a football team. Just like in football, I then had those teams square off against each other in a competition to see which team would prevail. These competitions led to two "conference champions" who would ultimately clash in the "Clean Energy Bowl." My great hope is that this analogy will make these big concepts more entertaining and at least somewhat easier to absorb.

This conference championship and Clean Energy Bowl framework will allow us to clearly determine the strengths and weaknesses of each team and come to a logical conclusion about which among them are in best position to change the world. After all, this is not a scientific exploration, but rather a big-picture kind of book that presents and compares only the most important concepts in clean energy.

I make this distinction because the data on many of these subjects changes almost daily. Sometimes this data can shift the specifics of the central debate. But what matters isn't the specifics—what matters is the viability and rationality of the framework for how to think about clean energy. If you have a framework, you can project the future instead of just sifting through a grab bag of loose facts. So while you might encounter a few data points that are slightly outdated by the time this book meets your hands, I'm confident that the framework and the conclusions to which it leads will remain relevant and insightful for years to come.

In many ways, I think the most important part of this examination of the future of clean energy is that set of comparisons between the teams, and how those teams may or may not impact the world in the near or distant future. Because I think that's the most important part—and because I'm trying to avoid getting too academic about every one of the hundreds of data points on the subject—I have to alert you to the fact that I sometimes use approximate or rounded numbers to explain my principles. Don't worry; I will cite the source so you can find the finer detail at your leisure. Keep in mind also that because we're talking about an ever-evolving topic here, those sources may not be as relevant to the specifics of this debate by the time you read them. My goal is to focus on the important overarching concepts and not a few decimal points of difference between Data Point A from the past and Data Point B from today.

So as we move forward, let's agree that this is not a scientific, deeply analytical book. As I say on the back cover, this book answers the energy sector's biggest questions in a way that anyone can understand and appreciate. We're not entering into a detailed debate over specific data about clean energy, after all. We're just two friends talking football (or future trends in clean energy). So let's get started.

The Clean Energy Bowl

What if I told you I had a system that could accurately predict which team would win the next Super Bowl? You'd want to place a bet immediately, wouldn't you? I know I would. Well, the odds makers can relax. I don't have such a system for football. But I think I *do* have a system that will accurately predict the winner in what I like to call "The Clean Energy Bowl."

With global warming and the environment being such hot topics today, there is a push to make America's future energy "clean." I put the word "clean" in quotes because "clean" is a relative term. There are many considerations that factor into whether and how you can deem an energy source "clean." For now, however, I'd like to concentrate on the two factors that will make an energy source the most likely to win in the next 20 years and beyond: (1) its ability to reduce particulate pollution and the emission of greenhouse gases, and (2) its positive impact on the world economy.

The environmental factor should be obvious. If the future of energy is indeed "clean," then the sources for energy that produce the lowest amount of particulate pollution and greenhouse gases should (*should*) be favored. But economics, as with anything in the United States, plays a huge role here too.

When I say *positive impact on the world economy*, I'm referring to many factors, but for now let's focus on the cost of producing and distributing energy. While it would be great if the cleanest energy sources were the most cost effective to implement, that's simply not always the case. As nice as it would be to say that we should just go with the cleanest technologies, the old adage remains true: money talks. So any reasonable examination of the future of clean energy must take into strong consideration the economic factors at play, as well.

Many people who speak about clean energy (or any energy) do so in a way that misrepresents its meaning. It's not unusual to hear a politician say something like, "We need more wind energy and solar energy so we don't have to import so much oil from other countries." But it's just not that simple. We're actually talking about two entirely different kinds of energy, and those different kinds of energy aren't directly related to one another. They belong to totally separate discussions.

One kind of energy is called *electricity.* This is the energy we use to power our homes and businesses and plug in all of our electrical equipment. The United States uses several sources to produce its electricity, including nuclear, wind, solar, water (which we sometimes refer to as hydroelectric power), geothermal, coal, and natural gas.

The other kind of energy is *fuel.* This is the energy we use to propel our cars, trucks, buses, trains, planes, and other vehicles. In the United States, the most common fuels are gasoline, ethanol, natural gas, diesel, and oil. Of that list, oil might stick out to you as one that doesn't necessarily belong. I place oil in with our discussion of fuels because a full 70% of the oil consumed in the United States is used for transportation fuel.* This makes it particularly important to evaluate within this category.

I digress. Back to the discussion about the difference between electricity and fuel. Think about it this way: when you plug your laptop into the wall, you're dealing with electricity. When you go to the gas pump to fill up your tank, you're dealing with fuel. Both of these things are kinds of energy, but they are almost completely unrelated to one another. Keep that distinction in mind, because it underlies the very framework of what we're going to be discussing in the pages to come.

Here's another important point: despite what some politicians might have you believe about their campaign platforms, the United States has

---

* Of that number, 46% goes to gasoline, 9% to airplane fuel, and 15% to diesel. The remaining 30% winds up as an ingredient in plastics and chemicals, including thousands of specific industrial products such as hand lotion, detergents, carpets, fertilizers, tires, trash bags, roofing, asphalt, clothing, safety glass, paint, and the list goes on and on and on. I mention all of this only to point out that oil is a complex subject, but for the purposes of this book, we'll be concentrating on its role as a contributor to American fuel. It's also worth pointing out that, in this context, the term "fuel independence" overlaps quite a bit with the term "oil independence."

already achieved energy independence when it comes to electricity. We can produce electricity from all the above-mentioned sources right here at home. All the coal, all the natural gas, all the nuclear, and so on, are produced right here on the continent and delivered to the end user by our own independent electrical grid. When people talk about the United States becoming energy independent, if they mention anything about coal, natural gas, wind, solar, water, geothermal, or nuclear power, then they're either confusing the issue or simply talking about the wrong things. We can make all the electricity we need without having to import it from other countries.

By deductive logic, we know that if a person is talking about energy independence, and if the United States is already electricity independent, then what that person is really talking about is *fuel* independence. We do indeed import much of our fuel from foreign countries, so we are *not* fuel independent. We are, however, *electricity* independent.

It is important to note that the participants in and eventual winner of the Clean Energy Bowl might not necessarily be dominant forces in the energy discussion *today*. But, based on the trends emerging from my research, I believe they will be the primary providers of electricity and fuel during the decades to come.

Now that we've taken care of all the housekeeping, let's move on to some football.

The Clean Energy League

Think of what you know about the National Football League (NFL). In its simplest description, it's a crowded field of 32 football teams. Those 32 teams are divided into two equal conferences, the National Football Conference (NFC) and the American Football Conference (AFC). Over the course of a long season and the playoffs, the two conferences each produce a champion. These two champions then square off against one another in the big game, the Super Bowl.

How these two teams get to the Super Bowl depends on a number of factors. Good teams must possess an efficient offense as well as a reliable defense. Team owners, general managers, and coaches also play a major role, as does the league commissioner.

Considering all these variables, it is virtually impossible at the start of the season to accurately predict which two teams will play in the Super Bowl. But thanks to advanced statistics, payroll allocations, and past performances, one can usually make an educated guess as to which teams have the best shot. The teams with the most dominant offenses and defenses often win. They get those dominant offenses and defenses by spending wisely on facilities, coaches, and players. And of course it always helps if they find themselves in a conference with weak competition.

Turns out, you can say many of the same things about clean energy. So let's imagine each clean energy source as we would an NFL team. There is Team Coal, Team Ethanol, Team Gasoline, Team Geothermal, Team Natural Gas, Team Nuclear, Team Solar, Team Water, and Team Wind, and they are all competing against one another in their respective conferences. Then, the winner of each conference plays in the Clean Energy Bowl. I'll discuss what it takes to win the Clean Energy Bowl in a moment, but for now, keep in mind that each team competes within its own conference first before earning that opportunity to become the overall champion.

Much like the NFL, our Clean Energy League divides into two conferences. That's because, as I mentioned in the introduction to this chapter, whenever we talk about energy in America, we're really talking about two separate and completely different categories. One category is electricity, or all the energy that the United States needs to power its millions of homes, factories, and businesses. The second category is fuel, or all the energy that the United States needs to power its millions of cars, trucks, and other vehicles. Whether solar wins the contest to provide electricity to the majority of US homes has no bearing on whether gasoline continues to be the primary provider of fuel for US vehicles, and vice versa.

For the purposes of our Clean Energy League, we must therefore place all energy sources that deal only with electricity into one conference and all energy sources that deal only with fuel into another.** Aligning them in this way will allow us to better predict which team makes the strongest case to be champion of America's future fuel needs and which team will provide the majority of America's future electricity needs. From there, one

---

** Note that natural gas has proven useful as both a fuel and electricity source, so I will include a discussion about this team in both leagues.

of those teams will emerge as the winner of the Clean Energy Bowl, and hence the energy provider that will make the most positive environmental and economic impact over the coming decades.

The Two Energy Conferences: Electricity Conference and Fuel Conference

As the title of this section suggests, we'll call the first conference the Electricity Conference. Each team in the Electricity Conference competes to become America's primary future source for powering homes and businesses. This conference is a crowded field with many strong teams. These include Team Wind, Team Solar, Team Water, Team Geothermal, Team Coal, Team Natural Gas, and Team Nuclear. Competition in the Electricity Conference has always been fierce, but recent trends suggest that one team may just be ready to start crushing the rest of the field.

We'll call the second conference the Fuel Conference. Each team in the Fuel Conference competes to become America's most environmentally sound and economically advantageous source for propelling its millions of vehicles. Unlike the Electricity Conference with its many strong teams, the Fuel Conference has always been dominated (and will continue to be dominated) by two exceedingly talented teams: Team Gasoline and Team Ethanol. There are other small teams in the field, certainly. For instance, some large buses and trucks use natural gas to power their engines. Some of the more adventurous car drivers have turned to natural gas, as well. This is because lately there's been a great deal of vertical and horizontal drilling and fracking to produce natural gas in large quantities. Natural gas as a fuel source does show some potential, but my ultimate conclusion is that it has too many flaws to compete long-term with Team Gasoline and Team Ethanol. In this conference, the data suggests that it would be foolish at this point to bet on anyone else.

Deciding Factors: The Electricity Conference

There are a few trends within our two conferences that will allow us to more easily determine the most logical choice for champions. For the electricity conference, they include:

1. Substantial competition exists.

For the purposes of our study, I intend to analyze seven potential sources for America's future electricity needs. With seven strong teams competing against one another, it will be difficult to predict a winner in this conference. Fortunately, some recent trends provide helpful insight as to the strongest teams.

2. Government subsidy is a fickle thing.

In this conference, the influence of the US government makes arriving at an accurate prediction even more difficult. To change the way the United States manages its electricity production would require a great deal of money, and it is often national, state, or local governments that supply that money. Different governmental leaders have different opinions on which electricity sources should receive that money at any given time.

For example, sometimes they favor wind power, and when that happens, Team Wind makes substantial gains in the standings. But then as soon as the next administration takes office, Team Wind might find its subsidies taken away and given to Team Nuclear. Its advantage is therefore lost.

For this reason, we must consider subsidies as advantages during certain times and as losses of advantage when they disappear. This means that, during the next 20 years, our best bet is to assume at least a relatively level playing field in regards to subsidy.

3. Global warming is very real.

Before we dive in, let's clear the air on a common misconception. There are two terms people use when they discuss the possibility that our planet has gotten warmer over the past several decades: *global warming* and *climate change*. Many people use these terms as if they are interchangeable, when in fact they mean different things.

Climate change refers to the long-term changes we can observe in the earth's average climate—and when I write "long-term," I mean *thousands* of years. When I write "changes we can observe," I mean increases *or* decreases in average temperature. Climate change can refer to the slow, natural drift in the earth's climate toward an ice age (when it gets so cold that much of the planet winds up covered in glaciers) or toward an interglacial age (like the one we've been experiencing for quite a long time).

The climate change phenomenon is caused by natural factors like an increase or decrease in solar radiation reaching the earth, plate tectonics, and even volcanic activity. There are many technical details, but the important takeaway message is that climate change is a natural occurrence that leads to prolonged periods of either warmer or colder average temperatures. This is why, when someone calls the rapid increase in average global temperatures that we have observed over the past century *climate change*, they're not calling it the right thing. The correct term is *global warming*.[1]

Global warming refers to the ongoing rise in the planet's average temperatures. Many people suggest that global warming is entirely manmade. This is because the rise in the planet's average annual temperatures has been unprecedented and rapid, and the only thing we know of that can account for such a drastic change are all those greenhouse gases mankind pumps into the atmosphere.[2] The latest data appears to render the rather fiery recent debate about global warming moot. Because the evidence is so compelling, we're going to accept that global warming is very real.[***][3]

At some point in another hundred years or less, the situation

---

[***] It was nice to think it possible that we've merely been witnessing entry into one of those interglacial periods presumably caused by (1) the earth moving from a circular to an elliptical orbit around the sun on about a 100,000-year cycle; (2) the earth being tilted in relationship to the sun, the tilt changing on about a 41,000-year cycle; and/ or (3) the earth wobbling slightly, the wobble changing on about a 26,000-year cycle. These cycles are known as Milankovitch cycles. I won't bore you with the details other than to say that when these changes line up in a certain way, they lead to an ice age, and when the opposite happens, we experience an interglacial age.

The Milankovitch cycles may or may not be reality, but what is reality is that the earth is currently warming at a relatively rapid pace. Typically these changes have occurred slowly, over 10,000 to 100,000 years. But over the past hundred years, global temperatures have increased much faster than we would expect if the natural Milankovitch cycles were the only factors at play.

may become catastrophic.[4] Of course, because we're not looking at anything that will adversely affect the majority of people in the immediate future, it's going to be quite difficult to get people to do anything to solve the problem. Think about it. How often do you spend money on something you know won't impact you personally for many years to come?

Take Christmas, for example. Because you know it's coming every year, you probably make preparations ahead of time to buy gifts for your loved ones. But what about retirement? You know it's coming, but because it is so distant and uncertain, you might be less inclined to save money for it right now. Maybe you do save for retirement. Maybe you're one of the people who acts on what you know is coming in the more-distant future and puts enough money away every month to expect a stable retirement. Good for you. Make no mistake, though: you're in the minority.[5] We've all heard about

---

For many years now, scientists have known that greenhouse gases in the atmosphere act to warm the earth. This is because, as they collect in the atmosphere, these gases trap the earth's heat, preventing it from escaping into space. Incidentally, this is just like what happens with clouds, which act to trap heat in the atmosphere. Without clouds, the earth is much cooler at night and much warmer in the daytime.

Unfortunately, with the continued accumulation of greenhouse gases, global warming may destabilize the earth's climate. While it is true that small amounts of greenhouse gases are released into the air as a result of natural activity, the overwhelming majority of the greenhouse gases currently collecting in the atmosphere are the result of human activity. Largely they come from the burning of coal, natural gas, and oil.

The global increase in mean temperature of about two degrees Fahrenheit during the past one hundred years is far greater than could be expected on the basis of natural climate change alone. The amount of carbon dioxide over the past 800,000 years, as measured by ice core samples, has ranged between 180 and 300 parts per million (ppm). During the peak of an ice age, it was 180 ppm. During the peak of an interglacial age, it got as high as 300 ppm, a number that coincided with the earth being as warm as it had ever been in the past 800,000 years. As of May 2013, the latest measurement of carbon dioxide in the atmosphere was an astounding 400 ppm, and the number is steadily increasing. What this means is that the earth is projected to become warmer than it has been for nearly 800,000 years.

For further reading on this subject, see endnote 4.

the importance of saving for retirement, but most people would prefer to spend the money on things that affect them immediately.

So how do we overcome this common human phenomenon? By preaching the importance of doing something about global warming? Preaching to people always sounds good to those doing it, but the impact it has on their audience is much, much less than if something actually happens to them. To paraphrase a famous line by President Lyndon Johnson, giving a speech is like peeing your pants. "It seems hot to you, but it never does to anyone else."[6]

When it comes to preaching the impact of global warming to the masses, you can call it similar to peeing your pants. You might have all the data in the world, but until global warming impacts everybody directly and immediately, it's unlikely that the average person will make any major lifestyle changes to combat it.

That's why it's so important to examine both the environmental and the economic impact of each team in this conference. The winner will cut down on pollution while providing affordable electricity to the mass market.

While most of the global warming figures forecast a bleak long-term scenario, the good news is that we can still head it off before it becomes a catastrophic problem, as long as we make some changes to the ways we consume electricity and fuel. Those changes are coming. Through our examination of each team and each conference, we'll figure out exactly which technologies will dominate that change effort.

4. We've got all the raw material we need.

Fully 27% of the world's coal supply lies within the boundaries of the United States.[7] That's a whole lot of coal. With a 250-year supply of coal left at current rates of use, the United States is truly the "Saudi Arabia of coal."[8] On top of that, the United States can count on 87 years of known natural gas reserves at current rates of use.[9] As for electricity produced by nuclear plants, there is sufficient uranium to keep the world in electricity for thousands of years.[10] Then you have wind, water, geothermal, and solar energy that can last virtually forever. In sum, we're talking about an adequate supply of electricity that we can produce right here at home.

None of the teams in the Electricity Conference will have to face the added stressor of competition from electricity imports. The United States has everything it needs to produce as much electricity as it wants, pretty much forever, available right here within its borders.

Whereas we could see a tremendous shakeup in the power structure of the Fuel Conference when the supply of oil drops and the price increases (probably substantially), there will never be any such concern in the Electricity Conference. This is primarily because, if one energy source fails to produce enough electricity, the six other energy sources can pick up the slack. Wind, solar, water, nuclear, and geothermal electricity will last as long as the earth itself. Even when the day comes that there is no coal or natural gas left to extract, people will have the other five teams on which to rely for their electricity needs.

To reiterate, the four deciding factors in the Electricity Conference are these:

1. The Electricity Conference is so crowded that it will be difficult to predict an absolute winner (though I have my theories).
2. Government subsidy is unpredictable and further clouds the picture.
3. Global warming is real and will impact future decisions in electricity policy.
4. Unlike in the Fuel Conference, there will never be a shortage of resources to make electricity in the Electricity Conference, meaning that there will be plenty of opportunity for each of our seven teams to compete.

Deciding Factors: The Fuel Conference

Stop me if you've heard this one. Two hikers wander off the trail, pushing through the foliage and making their way toward a stream. There, they stumble across a massive grizzly—and the bear doesn't take kindly to their intrusion. The grizzly stands up on its hind legs, growling and flashing its menacing claws. The two hikers turn and run. The bear gives chase. The hikers tear through the woods, leaping over logs and ducking branches. But the bear keeps gaining ground.

"We're never going to outrun that bear," one of the hikers says to the other.

"I don't have to outrun the bear," the other hiker says. "I just have to outrun you."

I love this anecdote, particularly as it applies to the power structure of the Fuel Conference. Unlike the Electricity Conference, where there are seven teams competing for the conference title, the Fuel Conference has only two truly viable teams: Team Gasoline and Team Ethanol."" Neither Team Gasoline nor Team Ethanol needs to worry about the other, more minor competing fuel sources. While it is true that neither team is perfect, it is also true that one simply has to be slightly better than the other in combined economic and environmental factors to be the winner. With just a slight advantage, one team will "run faster" and leave the other team to the bear.

1. The internal combustion engine (ICE) isn't going away.
I won't get into too much detail here on my findings regarding the future of cars and trucks. (I'll save that for chapter 7.) But if I'm going to make the claim that only two fuel sources will be viable, I should probably provide my primary reasoning. In short, there are only two practical fuels that work in the internal combustion engine: gasoline and ethanol.

Important Note #1: Yes, diesel works in the internal combustion engine. I've just chosen to lump it in with gasoline for the purposes of this study because it has roughly the same economic dynamics as gasoline. Just as importantly, it comes from the same source: oil.

Important Note #2: Yes, I'm aware that natural gas also works in an internal combustion engine. But the investment in infrastructure and other implementation changes necessary to make this a

---

"" As I mentioned, despite the recent boom, I don't believe natural gas to be a viable competitor as a fuel for cars in the United States.

completely viable alternative to gasoline would be staggering. The odds for this to occur are therefore quite low.

The number of vehicles in the world is expected to approximately double by 2030. At that time, 90% of the vehicles will use internal combustion engines. The other 10% will employ newer technologies such as hybrids, plug-in hybrids, and fully electric cars.[11] This means that the potential for economically favorable use of oil and ethanol will continue for at least the next 50 years or more.

2. Government subsidy is unpredictable.

The government used to give direct subsidies for building or expanding modern ethanol plants. Those subsidies have ended. Meanwhile, other subsidies are given to gasoline companies that blend and distribute ethanol. There is mounting pressure in congress to end those subsidies, but they still exist at the time of this writing. There is also mounting pressure to reduce the subsidies for oil, as well as for certain alternative-engine cars. I bring these points up because they suggest that we shouldn't be surprised if subsidies now given to a variety of energy producers will disappear.

I also bring them up because it's clear that if the mandate for ethanol and the huge subsidies for gasoline were both removed today, ethanol would find itself in the enviable position of being priced much lower than gasoline, its most formidable competition. This would make the demand for ethanol stunningly high. So if the subsidies for oil and gasoline suddenly ended, Team Gasoline would have to pull over for a pit stop while Team Ethanol raced on by. More on this subject in chapter 7.

3. Sustainability is important.

In any long-term prediction, the most important factor at play is sustainability. If an energy source is not renewable, then it has a finite lifespan. If it has a finite lifespan, then it cannot be considered the winner of the Clean Energy Bowl.

Team Gasoline is the current champion of the Fuel League. It may continue to be the champion for many years to come, but oil is a nonrenewable resource. That resource will dwindle eventually, and will dwindle rapidly as India, China, and various countries in Central America, South America, Africa, Southeast Asia, and much of the rest of the world develop their economies.[12] By the way, if China ever reaches the advanced industrial and technological level of the United States—and it is well on its way—it would, all on its own, consume almost all the oil now being produced in the world, leaving only a small amount for the other 194 countries.

Ever since 1970, we have seen a downward slide in the amount of new oil discovered globally, with an occasional upward bump when compared to the previous year (as is happening right now with shale oil). No matter what, we know that oil will eventually run out because it is a nonrenewable resource that took millions of years to make.

Ethanol, meanwhile, is produced in the United States from corn, a renewable resource generated by a new crop every year. As long as the United States has the ability to grow corn, it will be able to produce a fuel that will run its millions of internal combustion engines. Then again, even if the country can't grow enough corn to meet demand, science provides a new avenue: using dead plants or material left over from corn harvests, we can create something called cellulosic ethanol. This makes the product even more sustainable and renewable.

Advantage Team Ethanol.

4. The global economy plays a role.

In 2012, 50% of the oil the United States used was imported from foreign countries. The percentage of oil imported from foreign countries will decrease in the next ten years due to new shale oil in the United States. However, as we'll learn later, the amount of shale oil produced is going to be far, far less than some media moguls have claimed.

In 2030, after US shale oil closes in on the bottom of a severe downturn and then runs out, projections suggest that imports will soar to 75% of our oil use.[13] This looks certain to happen—and probably well before 2030. No matter what you believe about the date of the peak, a great many reputable people and groups are calling the recent spurt in US shale oil production a bubble, and one that will soon burst. In addition, there is substantial evidence that global conventional oil use has already peaked.*****

Meanwhile, OPEC (the Organization of Petroleum Exporting Countries, including Algeria, Angola, Ecuador, Iran, Iraq, Kuwait, Libya, Nigeria, Qatar, Saudi Arabia, United Arab Emirates, and Venezuela) controls 73% of world oil reserves. All the other oil-producing countries in the world combine to control the other 27% of reserves.[14] For this reason, OPEC will largely control the world price of oil (and therefore of gasoline).

Don't believe me? Then consider the end of 2014. Back then, despite a large world supply, OPEC decided not to cut production, as they would normally do, in an effort to keep their prices high. This decision resulted in a steep plunge for world oil prices. Conversely, if OPEC then decided to reverse that decision and significantly cut production, the price of oil would soar.

To reiterate, the four deciding factors for the Fuel Conference are:

1. The internal combustion engine will continue to dominate and give a huge advantage to Team Gasoline and Team Ethanol.
2. Government support for ethanol will eventually become unnecessary.
3. Sustainability is an enormous factor when it comes to long-term economic viability.

***** This might be a generous estimate, but the United States possesses four percent of total global reserves of oil, including realistic estimates of shale oil production. I write that it might be generous because, while some groups state higher numbers, many more project between 2.2% to 2.8% of world reserves. I place the number higher than just about everyone for two good reasons: first, I always try to look on the sunny side of life; second, what I want to show is that, even if the optimists are correct at four percent, the US will be going faster down the slide toward zero than ever as the shale oil bubble bursts in 2016 and the amount of conventional oil heads ever lower.

4. The issue of domestic versus foreign oil will play a major role in the years to come.

With all these deciding factors under our belt, we can move on to analyze the categories we use to evaluate each team's strengths and weaknesses, and then show how each team will fare within its respective conference.

CHAPTER 2

Determining the Conference Champions

W hile an NFL season spans a mere 20 weeks (including the playoffs), we won't know whether I've correctly picked the winners of the Clean Energy Conferences for up to 20 years from now (although there will certainly be strong indications before then). Even so, I invite you to place your bets now, as I am doing.

In hopes of helping you place the best bet, let's analyze the categories that inform us about each team's strengths and weaknesses. With this close study, we'll be able to assess which teams are in best position to become the primary providers of America's future electricity and fuel. If we can arrive at a pair of winners, we can then accurately predict which of the two will be the most economically viable and environmentally friendly over the next 20 years and beyond. This champion we will crown as the winner of the Clean Energy Bowl.

The Electricity Conference

The teams participating in this conference are Team Coal, Team Geothermal, Team Natural Gas, Team Nuclear, Team Solar, Team Water, and Team Wind. To repeat, just so it's clear, these are the four deciding factors that will dictate the outcome:

1. The Electricity Conference is so crowded that it will be difficult to predict an absolute winner (though I have my theories).
2. Government subsidy is unpredictable and further clouds the picture.

3. Global warming is real and will impact future decisions in electricity policy.

4. Unlike in the Fuel Conference, there will never be a shortage of resources in the Electricity Conference, meaning that there will be plenty of opportunity for each of our seven teams to win.

Since there are so many similarities between the teams in this conference, rather than running a team-by-team analysis, let's instead address categories that factor into each team's potential to win over the long term. We will divide the categories into offense (economic strength) and defense (environmental impact). In the end, this will allow us to arrive at a reasonable picture of which teams will be the strongest competitors in the conference.

Economic Viability (Quarterback)

The best football teams have great quarterbacks. In the Clean Energy League, the best teams are the most economically viable. Teams with poor economic factors are just like teams with bad quarterbacks: they will win games only if everything else (such as public support, technological advancement, and government subsidy) comes perfectly into alignment.

The teams with the best economic outlooks are Team Nuclear, Team Water, Team Coal, and Team Natural Gas. The teams with the worst economic outlooks (currently) are Team Wind and Team Solar. Without government subsidy and support, these two teams struggle due mainly to high production costs, massive use of land, and problems with transmission and storage. For now, Team Wind and Team Solar will have trouble winning any games without government help, but with new developments in technology, they might become formidable opponents. Wind, for instance, is making rapid progress, with solar lagging behind.

Team Nuclear has by far the best quarterback in the form of an emerging technology known as small modular reactors (SMRs). Before I get into detail on what an SMR is, I should probably point out what I mean when I use the term "reactor." We are, after all, going to be discussing both nuclear *plants* and nuclear *reactors* in the coming chapters, so it's important to know the difference. I'll be quick, I promise. It's really kind of simple anyway: a nuclear *reactor* is the vessel in which we place the nuclear fuel that winds up generating electricity; a nuclear *plant,* meanwhile, is the entire complex of buildings and land that houses a nuclear reactor. Even more simply: a nuclear plant is the complex in which you keep your nuclear reactor(s). A nuclear plant can house one reactor, two reactors, or even several reactors—and those reactors can be either the traditional or small modular reactor type.

Make sense? Okay, good. Then let's move on to how exciting SMRs are for the future of Team Nuclear.

First, what is a Small Modular Reactor? Well, its definition resides in its name. An SMR is *small* compared to traditional large nuclear reactors (the kinds you see with the big concrete cooling towers). It is also *modular,* meaning that the smaller size of the reactor and the nature of an SMR plant's infrastructure allow you to add additional reactors if your electricity production needs ever expand. And finally, it is a nuclear reactor, which is a technology capable of generating large amounts of low-cost electricity without producing any greenhouse gases.

Another particular strength of SMRs is their variable size. At their largest, an SMR can produce up to one-third the amount of electricity of a large nuclear reactor (again, the ones with the concrete cooling towers). Such an SMR can power as many as 300,000 homes. An SMR plant this size would occupy as much land as a large Walmart and its parking lots.[1]

SMRs can be much smaller, too. In fact, they can be as tiny as a hot tub. An SMR this size can provide electricity for 20,000 homes.[2]

Other advantages include the fact that SMRs are buried underground within a barrier of protective steel; they don't require refueling for up to ten years; they are constructed on factory assembly lines (which reduces cost); they can be shipped anywhere in the world; and they produce little waste.

Whereas before it cost billions of dollars to approve and build nuclear plants, SMRs offer a relatively low cost and significantly smaller size. Depending on the size of the reactor and the company that does the manufacturing, you can either receive a shipment of the parts and assemble it on-site or receive a prefabricated, working reactor from the manufacturing plant.[3] This potential makes them veritable game changers for Team Nuclear.

Cost per Household (Budget and Payroll)

In the NFL, the best teams tend to be the ones with well-managed budgets. You can say something similar of the Clean Energy League. If we remove from consideration the impact of global warming and other pollution issues, the teams with the highest cost per household are primed to lose to the teams with the potential to expand while also producing a low cost per household.

The chart below shows how each team currently performs in terms of cost per household:[4]

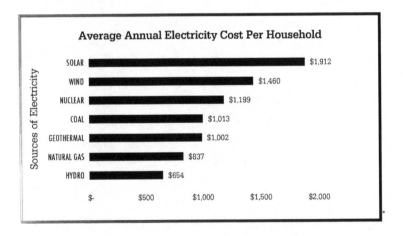

As you can see, Team Water (referred to above as "Hydro," meaning hydroelectric) is the low-cost producer of electricity, while Teams Solar, Wind, and Nuclear are higher cost, and Teams Coal, Geothermal, and Natural Gas reside in the middle. But with new

---

* The data presented in this table is continuously updated by a variety of organizations. One of the best-known organizations is the US Energy Information Administration. Their Annual Energy Outlook is available at http://www.eia.gov/forecasts/aeo/index.cfm.

advances in nuclear technology, we can anticipate a much, much brighter future for Team Nuclear.

In the short term, it appears that Team Natural Gas is making great strides in this category as well. This is in part because extraction capabilities have improved and in part because public sentiment toward this electricity/fuel source has gotten more positive. But those great strides may lead to some steps backward if current trends continue. New realities that allow for better and easier transport will take the commodity from a local product to a global one. Thanks to new techniques for converting natural gas to liquid natural gas (LNG), the commodity will soon enter the world market in a big way. Whereas before you could only use natural gas in the country of origin, LNG makes it possible to ship the product overseas. Given that the price for natural gas is currently so much higher in Asia and Europe than it is in the United States, US natural gas companies have a huge incentive to export to those continents. Eventually this will lead to a higher price per barrel for natural gas in the United States as well, because the price will be set by the world market instead of the local market.

Yes, the president can limit exports if he chooses, but he'll have to be willing to navigate the political pressure from producers. For these reasons, the brief advantage that Team Natural Gas enjoys in this category could disappear almost as quickly as it arrived.

When one looks at the extreme long term—say, a hundred or more years from now—coal, oil, and natural gas will have dried up completely. The only remaining sources of electricity will be water, solar, wind, geothermal, and nuclear. As you can see in the chart above, water is by far the most efficient of these. But there are three problems with water power. One is that you must be close to a source of moving water in order to efficiently receive the electricity produced by a hydroelectric plant. The second problem is that the number of dams that can be built is limited. We've just about dammed everything we can dam. The final problem is that there are environmental consequences to building a dam across a river.

Nuclear power, however, requires a much smaller amount of land than solar and wind, and it doesn't have the collection and transfer problems of renewable electricity producers like water.

Plus, the amount of land required for nuclear is shrinking further thanks to the aforementioned emerging technology, Small Modular Reactors (SMRs).

Transmission/Storage (Stamina)

The best teams in this conference should be able to deliver electricity to the public at the lowest possible cost. This is much like a football team's stamina. The best players on the good teams don't need to rest on the sidelines while the game marches on. Unfortunately for Team Solar and Team Wind, they tend to need far more rest than anyone else. While they're resting, the other teams are scoring at will. Conversely, the good energy providers are able to transmit enough power that they never have to temporarily stop producing electricity.

The table below shows which teams have transmission problems and which do not.

Transmission Problems	
YES	NO
Geothermal	Coal
Large Nuclear Reactors	Small Nuclear Reactors
Solar	Natural Gas
Wind	
Water	

Teams Wind and Solar only produce electricity part of the time. For all the reasons stated above, that makes them less competitive. These teams are trying to overcome that deficit by storing energy when the wind or the sun produce more power than is needed and then sending it into the grid while the sun isn't shining or the wind isn't blowing. So far, that power has proven difficult to store. In addition, producing enough wind or solar energy to power a city requires huge swaths of land, which means that solar and wind farms must be built far outside metropolitan areas. For this reason, they require long transmission lines, which can be costly and lead to power loss. The same problem applies to Team Water and Team Geothermal, given that their power generally must be transmitted long distances.

Reliability Factor

You can't win if you don't show up to play. *Reliability factor* refers to the ratio of an electricity source's actual output over a period of time versus its output if it were to produce electricity at one hundred percent of its potential in the same time frame. The lower the reliability factor, the less reliable or consistent the electricity source. Teams with low reliability factors will have a disadvantage because there will be times when they just don't show up to play.

The following table shows the breakdown of each team in the conference in terms of reliability factor.[**]

Reliability Factor	
Geothermal	92%
Nuclear	90%
Natural Gas	87%
Coal	85%
Water	52%
Wind	34%
Solar	25%

The thing to note here is that Teams Wind, Solar, and Water suffer from the lowest reliability factors. Team Solar, producing at

[**] This book takes the position that the sources of electricity listed in this table as "less reliable" will only become providers of large and reliable amounts of electricity if/when they become capable of *storing* amounts of electricity equivalent to that produced by a nuclear, natural gas, or coal-fired plant. In some cases, the costs associated with storing energy have recently come down, but storing energy from these sources still isn't cost effective enough to allow them to compete with nuclear, natural gas, and coal.

The currently less-reliable sources of electricity production are more likely to be used primarily for smaller applications than to power large swaths of the American electricity grid.

only 25% reliability, is by far the least reliable team in the conference. Teams Nuclear, Natural Gas, Coal, and Geothermal, meanwhile, can be counted on to play hard and produce well nearly all the time.

Perhaps the most important factor here is that nearly all the teams in this conference have reached their ceilings in terms of technology, Team Nuclear being the exception. Teams Wind and Solar may make some advances in the coming years, but not on the level of the advances we have seen and will continue to see for Team Nuclear. SMRs in particular make Team Nuclear's reliability factor the steadiest, most dependable, and most bankable in both the short and long term.

Environmental Impact (Defensive Efficiency)

Perhaps the best way to judge a football team's defense is through its overall ability to shut down opposing offenses. Similarly, the best way to judge a Clean Energy Team's defense is through its ability to produce electricity without causing harm to the environment via airborne particulates, greenhouse gases, water contamination, or toxic waste that is not securely stored.

The following table ranks each team in terms of harmful impact on the environment.

Negative Environmental Impact	
YES	NO
Natural Gas	Wind
Coal	Solar
	Geothermal
	Nuclear
	Water

Obviously, Teams Natural Gas and Coal are the only teams in the conference that are not by definition "clean." Both have made advancements recently that allow them to generate electricity while releasing lower amounts of particulate matter, greenhouse gases, or other pollutants, but the gap between their environmental impact and that of the other teams remains substantial.

Two of the more controversial teams in terms of environmental impact are Team Nuclear and Team Water. While nuclear power produces few if any airborne particulates, it does generate relatively small amounts of toxic waste, and that can be a hot-button issue with environmentalists. Fortunately for Team Nuclear, recent technological advances make it possible to recycle nuclear waste into new nuclear fuel. This technology dramatically reduces nuclear waste and can even help reduce waste which has already been stored. Many nations already use this technology safely and effectively, and even though the US is not currently using it, it has the ability to adopt the technology as well.[5] For these reasons, the time will soon come when we can think of Team Nuclear in the same light, pollution-wise, as clean teams like Team Wind and Team Solar.

Team Water, meanwhile, holds all the same zero-emissions and zero-contaminants advantages as Teams Solar, Wind, and Geothermal, but it does occasionally have an impact on the environment. Most hydroelectric plants require large dams in order to function. While large areas of still water can be great for boating and swimming, they can also damage the local ecosystem. Algae often thrive in these areas, and algae tend to raise water temperature, which alters the delicate balance of these fragile water habitats. Dams also disrupt the migration patterns of certain fish. Then, if they break, it can lead to catastrophe for animals and humans alike, but I'll get into that in a later chapter.

Overall, the clear winners in the environmental category are Teams Wind and Solar. But given the dismal offenses displayed by both these teams, strong defense alone will not win many games. Thanks in part to advances in nuclear technology, Team Nuclear is one of the better teams in this category.

And one final note: if global warming turns out to have severe near-term consequences, a responsive government will be inclined to turn rapidly to an alternative clean technology that can (1) produce massive amounts of clean and reliable energy, and (2) be implemented seamlessly into the portion of the electrical grid currently powered by coal plants.[6] This is where Team Nuclear and SMRs will gain the most ground. What better way to quickly replace coal power at a relatively low cost than with power plants that can occupy the same or less space, power the same number of homes or more, and do so without creating particulate pollution and greenhouse gases? There is literally no electricity need the world over that we can't meet with next-generation nuclear plants.

Who Will Win the Electricity Conference?

The main problem with predicting the outcome of the Electricity Conference with absolute certainty is that there are just so many teams in play. Each team has tremendous strengths and staggering weaknesses. In the short term, some teams will win in certain years while other teams will win in other years. In the end, there will be so much demand for electricity—and so many sources available to provide that electricity—that it might not matter. It could be that no true winner emerges in the Electricity Conference in the shorter term, and that each team takes a certain percentage of market share.

Over the next few years, state and local governments will continue to influence the outcome of the Electricity Conference. Many government entities try to set prices for electricity in ways that allow people access to the cheapest possible electricity. To meet this end, these governments will continue to draft policy that will prevent electricity companies from charging too much.

As the United States grows in population and electricity consumption, the demand for additional energy will likewise grow so much that all teams will contribute at some level. Many teams will have the opportunity to succeed—and for that very reason, many teams *will* succeed if they are economically sound or subsidized by the government.

Betting on any single team in the Electricity Conference to win decisively in the short term would be a long shot. With a cloudy future, government intervention and control, environmental considerations, and an unpredictable economic outlook, there are simply no guarantees.

In the longer term, however, I think there is no question that one team will emerge victorious. At first, Team Nuclear might find it difficult to overcome its negative image with regard to safety—even though detractors base these faulty perceptions on past occurrences and older models of nuclear plants. These same detractors appear to have virtually no knowledge of the safety and efficiency of the latest generation of nuclear reactors. When Team Nuclear does manage to overcome its outdated image, it will find itself in perfect position to win the conference. The price of natural gas will climb again from its recent fracking supply boom lows. Coal will lose more ground due to its environmental impact. Solar and wind will continue to struggle to produce the massive amounts of electricity necessary to run a large electric grid.[***] And as all this is happening, Team Nuclear (with its technological progress) will take hold as the top team in the conference.

The interesting thing? The balance of power in the conference may already be shifting. In spite of continued scare tactics on the part of the media, those who understand the real story are moving ahead rapidly to build new nuclear plants worldwide. These backers apparently know of the safety of the latest generation of nuclear plants, the effectiveness of nuclear power in producing massive amounts of reliable, low-cost electricity, the virtually unlimited supply of low-cost fuel to run the plants, the innovations in recycling waste into new fuel, the development of SMRs, and the tremendous benefit of releasing virtually no greenhouse gases in the process.

Just to whet your appetite for the kinds of things I'm talking about, the chart below shows information on current and future nuclear plants in four major countries.

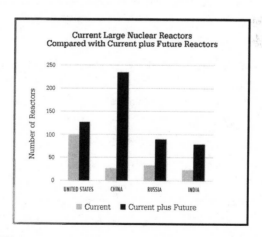

_____

[***] There is only one wind farm in the US that produces as much electricity as a large nuclear reactor. Wind and solar will continue to have problems with massive land use, transmission, storage, low reliability, and subsidy reduction.

Over the past 54 years, the world's many countries have constructed 438 large nuclear reactors.[7] That's an average of eight per year. But a compilation of worldwide data shows that, by 2030, the number of new nuclear reactors built worldwide will jump by 565, making a total of 1,003 large nuclear reactors worldwide.

The reasons for this projected expansion are simple, but let's return to the football analogy to make the point. At present, all the teams appear to be at least somewhat competitive in terms of size, strength, speed, skill set, economic viability, and so on. Going forward, all the teams will remain at or near their respective current levels in size, strength, speed, skill set, economic viability, and so on, save one: Team Nuclear.

With the projected and very real advancements in nuclear technology in place and on the horizon, we can expect Team Nuclear to get bigger, faster, and stronger every year. Eventually, it will be bigger, faster, stronger, and also smarter than any other team in the league. Leading the players all the while will be their tremendous quarterback: small modular reactors (SMRs), whose extraordinary power, low-cost design, assembly-line-production capabilities, and space-saving potential will consistently serve as game changers for Team Nuclear.

As recently as two years ago, I might not have been so sure about the winner in this crowded field. But as the smartest investor in technology stocks knows, it's not wise to choose a winner based on how good the company is now. Instead one must pay attention to the ability and opportunity the company has to be increasingly better in the future. With the latest data at hand, I feel comfortable projecting that in the Electricity Conference, Team Nuclear will be the winner.

Now that we've predicted the champion of the Electricity Conference, we can move on to our discussion of the winner of the Fuel Conference. This discussion will be substantially briefer, I promise, because there are really only two teams in the conference capable of competing year in and year out.

The Fuel Conference

Before we get into the nuts and bolts of this conference, please allow me to reiterate an important point: I recognize that gasoline and diesel are marketed and sold as different fuel products. I choose to tie them together into one team, Team Gasoline, for this study because they share roughly the same economic dynamics, and because they are both derived from oil.

Also, a disclaimer: for the remainder of this book, whenever I use the term *cars*, what I am referring to is any vehicle used to transport people and/ or goods over the road from one place to any other place the road will take them. That includes sedans, SUVs, pickups, station wagons, vans, and any other vehicles.

I'll also reiterate the deciding factors that will dictate the outcome of the Fuel Conference:

1. The internal combustion engine will continue to give a huge advantage to Team Gasoline and Team Ethanol.
2. Government support and mandates for ethanol will eventually become unnecessary.
3. Sustainability is an enormous factor when it comes to long-term viability.
4. The issue of domestic versus foreign production will play a major role in the years to come.

Since the continued domination of the internal combustion engine allows only two teams to remain competitive, let's examine Teams Gasoline and Ethanol in terms of their strengths and weaknesses. In this way, we will be able to conclude which of them has the advantage in the long run and is therefore most likely to win this conference and make it to the Clean Energy Bowl.

Team Gasoline

Economic Strengths
- Internal combustion engines boast one hundred years of research and development when it comes to the question of how to use gasoline most efficiently. These engines are constantly improving and getting more miles per gallon with the application of technological innovations.[8]
- There is already a nationwide infrastructure in place for refining oil into gasoline, blending it with ethanol, and delivering it to the estimated 121,466 gas stations all across the country.[9]

Environmental Strengths
- None.

Economic Weaknesses
- Virtually all of the profit in the gasoline business goes to the people who drill the oil out of the ground.
- As the consumer of 20% of the oil in the world, the United States has an interest in keeping the world price of oil down.[10] Since much of the oil it consumes comes from foreign countries, the US commits billions of dollars to maintain peace in the countries that can ensure them a continuous supply of oil.
- Compliance with important environmental and other regulations for building and operating an oil refinery is expensive, as is the overall cost of building a refinery. For these reasons, gasoline made outside the United States is cheaper. US refining margins are extremely thin. This is one reason why only 7 out of the 140 refineries currently operating in the US were built in the last 35 years.[11]
- Price competition among gas stations results in thin profit margins. This is why fully 82% of gas stations have convenience stores attached. If they don't give their customers an opportunity to purchase comparatively higher-profit items like food, beverages, and sundry household goods, station owners have trouble turning a decent profit.[12]

Environmental Weaknesses
- Gasoline exhaust is one of the world's highest contributors of harmful airborne particulates.
- In addition to the greenhouse gases produced, gasoline exhaust contains benzene, which can cause cancer.
- When spilled, gasoline can contaminate the ground and water.
- When spilled, gasoline is an extremely volatile fire hazard.
- Oil spills can have a devastating impact on the environment.

Overall

Team Gasoline is the heavy hitter in this league at present, but due to its negative environmental impact and the approaching decline in the world's supply of oil, the tide will eventually turn against it.

Team Ethanol

Economic Strengths

- The raw material for ethanol in the United States is corn, and in Brazil, sugarcane. Since ethanol is made from renewable commodities, it can be produced forever. That's a huge advantage over gasoline, which is made from a nonrenewable commodity that will someday run out.
- Ethanol lessens the need for oil imports. Less oil imported, particularly when OPEC controls the price of the import in question, always strengthens the American economy.
- The ethanol industry provides jobs and income for Americans. Corn cultivation, ethanol plant construction, ethanol refining, and ethanol distribution all add up to extraordinary job-creation potential.
- Ethanol enables progress toward US fuel independence.
- Reliance on ethanol reduces the amount of money paid for oil imports from countries known to support terrorist activity, and from other countries supporting ideologies that oppose those of the US.
- There is plenty of land available in the world to grow enormous additional amounts of corn and sugarcane.
- The southern United States could easily produce sugarcane-based ethanol in addition to corn-based ethanol.
- Ethanol biorefineries can be adapted to produce another renewable fuel, butanol, which has applications in useful chemical compounds.
- As byproducts of ethanol production, distillers grain is a significant high-protein livestock feed, and corn oil can be refined into biodiesel fuel.

Environmental Strengths

- Since it can produce 59% less greenhouse gas and particulate pollution than gasoline, ethanol's exhaust is much cleaner.[13]
- Ethanol contains no benzene. Benzene, which can cause cancer, is a chemical substance found in both gasoline and cigarette smoke.[14]
- When spilled on land, ethanol evaporates, leaving no trace at all.
- When spilled in water, ethanol likewise evaporates, as ethanol is pure alcohol.
- Less greenhouse gas is emitted during production of ethanol than during production of gasoline.
- If the production process for cellulosic ethanol becomes economically feasible, then one day it will be possible to make ethanol from nonfood waste materials like corn stalks, corncobs, trees, and some other carbon-based materials.

Economic Weaknesses

- As with gasoline, ethanol distributors make thin margins.
- As with gasoline, gas stations selling ethanol must rely on resultant concessions sales to turn a profit.
- Economic success currently depends largely on the price of gasoline being higher than the price of ethanol.
- Like gasoline, ethanol is heavily regulated by the government.
- Ethanol production is currently at a higher level than it would be otherwise due to government support and specific mandates for its production and use.

Environmental Weaknesses

- Ethanol exhaust contains some harmful particulate matter and greenhouse gases. However, it is much cleaner and safer than gasoline exhaust.

Overall

Team Ethanol has the clear advantage over Team Gasoline.

Who Will Win the Fuel Conference?

There are three factors at play that suggest to me that Team Ethanol will become far more likely to win (from an environmental and economic point of view) than Team Gasoline.

The first is that, from an environmental perspective, ethanol is much cleaner than gasoline. While it is true that the exhaust from both fuel sources produces harmful substances, it is also true that gasoline's exhaust is worse. Again, I remind you of the bear story. In terms of environmental impact, Team Ethanol merely has to be somewhat better than Team Gasoline because, from a practical standpoint, they are the only two fuel sources that make sense for the internal combustion engine. As a benefit in this category, the manufacture of ethanol at a processing plant produces no waste and no pollutants, while an oil refinery making gasoline releases a number of harmful pollutants and waste.

The second and more important factor is that oil is nonrenewable. Therefore, at some point, world production of oil will decline. Sooner than many people think, production will fail to meet demand at a historically reasonable price, especially when the shale oil bubble pops. And when that happens, the price of gasoline will rise.

Third, because corn is a renewable resource, it will be possible to make ethanol forever. The United States has plenty of land upon which to produce the corn necessary to meet present demand for ethanol. Further, because of technological advances, bushels-per-acre yield is expected to increase so dramatically that, by 2030, we'll be able to produce twice as much corn on the same amount of land.[15] Other countries will produce more corn as well, thereby increasing the total amount of corn available for ethanol worldwide.

As oil becomes scarcer and more expensive, Team Ethanol will find itself in excellent position to build a monopoly on fuel. As the price of gasoline increases, ethanol will become much less expensive than gasoline. That will make it possible to sell ethanol for a lower price than gasoline, benefiting consumers as well as the overall economy. The major advantage ethanol enjoys is that it is the *only* practical fuel beside gasoline that can power the internal combustion engine. For this reason, as world oil demand continuously grows and gasoline prices soar, ethanol will stand alone as champion in the Fuel Conference. No other fuel source will be able to compete.

So now we believe we know who our two conference champions will be: Team Nuclear in the Electricity Conference and Team Ethanol in the Fuel Conference. If we hope to arrive at a logical answer to which of these two conference champions will win the Clean Energy Bowl, we must first take an in-depth look at the advantages and disadvantages of each.

Over the next three chapters, I will outline a detailed argument for why I believe Team Nuclear to be a tremendous competitor for American (and world) electricity production, thereby making it a worthy opponent to Team Ethanol in the ultimate showdown.

For the four chapters thereafter, I will make a similar argument for why Team Ethanol is a virtual lock to unseat Team Gasoline as the longtime champion of the Fuel Conference, making it a tremendous competitor for the future of American (and world) fuel production and a worthy opponent to Team Nuclear.

So let us begin with our examination of nuclear power, kicking off with three advantages for nuclear energy as a future electricity source: cost, safety, and more efficient construction.

The Nuclear Awakening

Nuclear energy is the solution to all electricity problems in the world. That's a bold statement, but I intend to spend the next three chapters explaining why I feel so confident in this proclamation. Nuclear energy provides a clear answer to US and world needs for efficiency, low energy costs, safety, and reduction in greenhouse gases as well as other agents that lead to global warming.

There are three major hurdles for Team Nuclear to clear if it hopes to run away with the conference. The first is that it must find ways to overcome the mistaken belief that it is somehow a "dirty" electricity source because of the waste it produces. The second is that it must dispel fears about its safety. The third involves economic factors like the relatively high cost of production and the slow regulatory process the government requires in order to ensure that every nuclear plant operates effectively and safely.

If Team Nuclear manages itself well through all of those twists and turns, then it will surely be the winner in this conference and one of the most important technologies we have against the advance of global warming.

The strange thing about nuclear energy is that many people think of it as a dinosaur. They have this mistaken notion that *we tried that already, and it's scary, so we'd better try a safer way to produce electricity.* This misconception seems to be based on memories of wildly exaggerated reports surrounding events like Chernobyl, Three Mile Island, and Fukushima. Memories of these events have people thinking that there is no such thing as a safe nuclear plant.

There are 438 nuclear reactors operating in the world today.[1] Those 438 reactors provide approximately 13.5% of the world's electricity.[2] Thanks in part to the operation of these plants and in part to recent developments in nuclear technology, safety concerns are now practically irrelevant.

Further, there is an exciting new technology that will make nuclear power substantially safer, more cost effective, easier to implement in all corners of the globe, and wildly competitive in the race to provide electricity to all the newly developing countries worldwide.

Nuclear power is no dinosaur; it is the cutting edge of the future of electricity. The future of nuclear energy is far more efficient. The future of nuclear energy is clean. The future of nuclear energy has a far smaller geographic footprint. The future of nuclear energy is to provide the bulk of electricity to the majority of the globe. Read on to discover how.

Introducing the New Nuclear

When most people think about nuclear power, they picture those giant towers puffing endless clouds of steam into the air. For many decades, this is exactly what nuclear power was, for better or worse. Sure, it was an absolutely clean source of electricity in terms of air pollution, but people doubted its safety, it took up so much space, it dominated otherwise pristine horizons, and it produced all that problematically toxic waste.

None of these things is true of modern nuclear plants. We've recently entered a renaissance for nuclear power, yet many people seem to want only to hold Team Nuclear to mostly ill-founded beliefs about its past. That's exactly what we're not going to do here. Here, we're going to look into nuclear power's remarkable present and then gaze ahead to its bright future in American and global electricity production.

The bottom line is that the most modern nuclear plant designs have quietly made strides to reduce concerns about cost. There was a time when it cost too much to build and implement any nuclear plant without money or loan guarantees from the government. Not anymore. There was a time when nuclear plants represented such devastating potential to threaten public safety that a massive marketing campaign was required just to get voters to approve the construction of one of those big plants anywhere near their homes. Not anymore. There was a time when every nuclear plant had to be designed from scratch in order to meet the unique needs of the region it would serve, which only added to the up-front cost. Not anymore.

While the largest nuclear plants still require government funding or loan guarantees, the new SMRs are well within reach of private industry funding. As of now, the United States finds itself in prime position to roll out these new SMRs on assembly production lines, just as we currently do with cars and airplanes. Many other countries already have the ball rolling on this very concept. And very soon, these new SMRs will make it possible for every country—developed, developing, or undeveloped—to provide access to clean, safe, and cost-competitive electricity to all of its people. Imagine the economic growth that could create!

Nuclear Plants Sprouting Up Like Weeds

Quick: what's the best way to trigger rapid and sustained economic growth? Ensure that, every year, there are more people in position to buy things than there were in the year before. That's the simplest economic principle there is, as it derives directly from the concept of supply and demand. If your economy is slumping, it's slumping mostly because you don't have enough people buying goods and services. The best way to turn that boat around is to enable more people to buy goods and services. This is one part of Team Nuclear's attractiveness as a potentially dominant team in the Electricity Conference. If the world embraces nuclear power's present and near-future technologies, it will enable somewhere between 1.5 billion and 3 billion new electricity customers to step into the modern world. As they enjoy their new access to electricity, their standard of living improves. As their standard of living improves, they find themselves with more time to earn money, which in turn allows them to purchase more of the gadgets, cars, and luxuries that make the developed world what it is today.[3] That's a whole lot of new wallets ready to open to a new and unprecedented era of economic expansion.

The next component of Team Nuclear's attractiveness is that it creates electricity without releasing greenhouse gases into the air—a matter that's critical to the fight against global warming. World-Nuclear.org recently released a study called "Nuclear Century Outlook" in which they examine Team Nuclear based on exactly these two criteria: nuclear power's projected global growth in the twenty-first century, and nuclear power's potential contribution to the reduction of greenhouse gases.[4] What the study found is that we can project the number of nuclear plants in operation worldwide to increase exponentially in the coming century. As the title to this section suggests, new nuclear plants are going to begin sprouting up like weeds.

But let's start with that number I cited in the introduction to this section, because it surprises most people. We know that there are 438 nuclear plants in operation in the world today. Since we're talking about a 54-year history of nuclear power, that's an average of eight new plants constructed worldwide each year. Those plants provide 13.5% of all electricity to the planet at the time of this writing. That's a pretty remarkable set of figures. In the coming years, given the economic and environmental pressures at hand, those numbers are almost certain to go up.

According to the study, even the larger, more costly nuclear reactors are projected to increase significantly in number between now and the year 2100. The midrange projection from the study suggests that there will be as many as 6,880 large reactors in the world by that distant year, and the study's highest projection claims as many as eleven thousand. If you're doing the math, that's an average of over 120 new nuclear reactors per year for the next 87 years. It certainly is a high number, but that's what the study says will be needed to serve an increased population, as well as replace current coal plants and other less-efficient electricity producers.

What about nuclear expansion in the nearer decades? By 2030, the projection suggests that we will have more than doubled the total number of nuclear plants in the world, to about one thousand. By 2040, that number will double again. The curve continues to rise rapidly into the horizon of the year 2100. Even if we take the study's lowest-level estimate, we're still talking about more than two thousand new large reactors by the year 2100. That would represent "a five-fold increase over today's nuclear capacity."[5]

None of this takes into account the potential impact of small modular reactors (SMRs) either. It's possible that some of those projected large-scale plants could be replaced by SMRs. This could mean even more than the two thousand new plants projected to exist worldwide by the year 2100, as SMRs are more cost-effective and far simpler to construct compared to their large-scale nuclear plant counterparts.

The process has already begun. Many countries, the United States included, have recently ramped up their efforts to approve and construct large-scale nuclear plants. In fact, in 2012, "The US Nuclear Regulatory

Commission approved licenses to build two new nuclear reactors... the first authorized in over 30 years."[6]

This development is merely a harbinger of things to come for Team Nuclear. If plants are being approved and constructed once more after a 30-plus-year hiatus, then what we're seeing is a sea change in perspective on the technology. And according to the study, the more apparent and dangerous global warming becomes, the more rapid will be this change. "With 60 reactors being built around the world today, another 150 or more planned to come online during the next 10 years, and over two hundred further back in the pipeline, the global nuclear industry is clearly going forward strongly."[7]

A Question of Practicality

As of 2011, there were just over one hundred nuclear reactors in operation in the United States (104, to be exact), providing 20% of US electricity.[8] Many have suggested that the reason these numbers are not higher is that the cost for startup is just too impractical. This despite the fact that (1) "Nuclear power remains one of the only carbon-free base load power sources currently available,"[9] (2) "To accomplish the needed CO_2 emissions cuts to keep warming no greater than 2°C, the IEA says global nuclear power generation capacity needs to increase to 930 gigawatts from 396 gigawatts by 2050,"[10] and (3) "The nuclear energy industry is an engine for job creation and America's economic growth."[11]

It is true that a nuclear plant represents a high initial construction cost. This is in part due to the sophistication of its technologies, the many hurdles that stand in its way (some owed to public misperception of the relative safety of nuclear energy), and a need to institute safety standards that simply don't apply to other technologies.

At the same time, Team Nuclear crushes the competition in terms of reliability. As far as environmental practicality goes, there is really no contest. There are no other teams in the Electricity Conference that can produce such efficient, clean energy on such a large scale. In 2009 alone, nuclear power plants operating in the United States prevented the release of 647 million metric tons of CO_2. That's the equivalent of all the CO_2 emitted by every single passenger car in the United States. That's a whole lot of harmful greenhouse gas that didn't make it into our atmosphere because of nuclear power.

If nuclear power, even at its present capacity, has the ability to prevent as much pollution as we produce every year with our cars alone, imagine how much carbon dioxide emission we can prevent if the number of nuclear plants in operation rises on the curve suggested by the study.

For those who still think nuclear power isn't practical when it comes to fighting global warming, consider this: a study done by the University of Wisconsin showed the environmental life-cycle impact of nuclear energy is among the lowest of all forms of electricity generation. Nuclear energy is actually comparable to renewables such as wind and geothermal. Nuclear is an ultraclean technology that produces electricity at an amazingly efficient and cost-effective rate. So in terms of overall performance, there's really no better team in the conference.

Extraordinary Potential for Improvement

Nuclear energy has virtually unlimited potential for technological progress. When Einstein and others discovered a way to use the uranium atom to transform mass into energy, that moment represented a landmark achievement in science that far surpassed anyone's imagination. Since then, the advancements in the technology have been staggering, but even now, no one knows the limits to the potential for nuclear power.

It is my strong belief that, in terms of technological advancement, nuclear power has substantially higher potential for improvement than the other clean technologies in the conference. We're going to ignore the dirty technologies like coal and natural gas for the moment for two reasons: (1) they're nonrenewable, so their long-term future is limited, (2) they're dirty, so global warming will become a greater and greater problem for them in the coming years, and (3) with their centuries-old head start, they are already much further along in their technology-advancement life cycle.

So that leaves the other clean sources: solar, wind, geothermal, and water. These are the renewable energy sources that are still new enough that we can expect some measure of technological advancement in coming years. Never mind that they are already well behind Team Nuclear in efficiency and reliability; it remains possible they could see some advances in efficiency in the coming years. But as I will demonstrate in the next few paragraphs, those technological breakthroughs will pale in comparison to what we're already seeing in the exciting Team Nuclear camp.

When it comes to the other clean teams in the conference, the problem boils down to this: no matter how we improve the efficiency of a wind turbine, the technology still depends on the wind actually blowing enough to meet quotas for electricity; no matter how effective dams become, it's still expensive and inefficient to send hydroelectric power over great distances from dam to city; and no matter how advanced solar panels become, the sun still has to shine if they're going to work. The ceiling for each of these renewable technologies is pretty apparent. It's only as high as the wind, the water, or the sun will take it.

Team Nuclear, meanwhile, suffers from no such limitations. Take for instance the invention of breeder reactors. Proponents of nuclear technology saw shortcomings in the electricity source—namely, that it depended on uranium, a finite resource, to generate the power, and that power generation led to the potentially untenable byproduct of nuclear waste. Additionally, large reactors didn't use nearly as much of the energy potential of their fuel as they could have. In response, scientists invented breeder reactors, a new way to produce nuclear energy that cuts these waste and uranium-supply problems almost completely out of the equation.* "Breeder reactors could in principle extract almost all of the energy contained in uranium... decreasing fuel requirements by a factor of 100."[12]

Oh, there's also this:

> Breeder reactors could, in principle, extract almost all of the energy contained in uranium or thorium, decreasing fuel requirements by a factor of 100... The high fuel efficiency of

---

* As a disclaimer, I should mention two things. First, the concept of a breeder reactor, which produces little waste, has been around since the 1960s. Second, the reason we don't see more of them in operation today is because the need for them was superseded by the discovery of greater uranium reserves than anticipated. At present we don't really need breeder reactors because there is so much uranium. But if we ever do decide that we need them, they're already a viable technology.

breeder reactors could greatly reduce concerns about fuel supply or energy used in mining. Adherents claim that with seawater uranium extraction, there would be enough fuel for breeder reactors to satisfy our energy needs for 5 billion years at 1983's total energy consumption rate, thus making nuclear energy effectively a renewable energy. [13]

When compared to another clean energy like solar power, this kind of advancement is akin to inventing a second sun or learning to harness and control weather patterns to ensure that it's always sunny over our solar farms. While these other major renewable-resource teams depend on an unreliable and limited supply of their respective energy source, Team Nuclear has a virtually limitless supply of a resource that will keep it running for as long as this planet exists.

Small Modular Nuclear Reactors (SMRs) Will Change the World

I fully accept the notion that there are other obstacles standing in the way of Team Nuclear's dominance. This isn't just a matter of overcoming media misconceptions and establishing technology that will make nuclear power supersede the advantages of other renewable electricity sources. Some of the other obstacles include the money, resources, and time required to gain government approval; the cost and space requirements for constructing a large nuclear plant; the general eyesore quality of cooling towers; and questions of safety. I'll get deeper into the safety issue in the next chapter, but for now, let's talk about a technology that will render the other issues virtually irrelevant.

The SMR is not new technology. In fact, small reactors of this nature have been powering seaborne vessels like ships and submarines since 1950. Since then, 700 such reactors have been used at sea. At the time of this writing, a total of 200 reactors are in operation in seaborne vessels. In fact, all of the US Navy's submarines and aircraft carriers are nuclear powered. [14] So that's well over 60 years of experience powering some of the most important vessels in the US Navy. As SMRs move toward development for nonmilitary applications, their potential to change the game for Team Nuclear is truly amazing.

You probably recognize the above as a traditional large nuclear power plant. This one has two cooling towers (labeled with a "1" in the image above). A cooling tower cools the water and steam that have come through the generator to produce electricity. When the water has been cooled sufficiently, it is recycled back into the reactor's water supply.

The containment structures for the two reactors in this plant are labeled with a "2" in the image above. A containment structure is a 14-foot-thick combination of concrete and steel designed to prevent any radiation from ever escaping into the environment from the reactor and to protect the reactor from terrorist attack, whether by ground or by air.

Large nuclear power plants can have one, two, three, or even four reactors, but almost all of them have either one or two. We'll get into the makeup of a reactor a little later, but for now, let's focus on the sheer size of the plant pictured above. You'll note the cows in the foreground, there to give you a sense of the scale. If you've ever driven near one of these large nuclear plants, you know how they can dominate a skyline.

Now, compare that image to this one of a fully constructed and fully functional SMR:

Small Modular Reactor

As you can see, where before nuclear power depended on big, expensive plants that loomed large over skylines and demanded significant swaths of land, now you can fit an SMR on the back of a semi-truck. The places you could put a nuclear plant of this small size (including underground and almost completely out of sight) are numerous in comparison to the old, gigantic plants. In fact, while a large nuclear power plant can eat up one to two square miles of real estate, the largest current SMRs (capable of serving 300,000 people) occupy about the same amount of space as your local Walmart.[15] This opens up a whole world of possibilities in terms of location, construction feasibility, and nearby access to electricity for homes and businesses.

Whenever I think about SMRs, I conclude that there are many, many reasons they'll change the game in the Electricity Conference. For the purposes of this chapter, however, I've distilled those reasons down to six.

1. No greenhouse gases.

We've discussed this point already, but it bears repeating (probably again and again): nuclear power, no matter how you slice it, produces no greenhouse gases.** Small though they are, SMRs share all the advantages of large nuclear plants—namely, they can produce electricity more reliably than technologies like wind and solar power while generating virtually none of the greenhouse gases attributed to coal and natural gas. This positions SMRs nicely as a future key contributor for Team Nuclear, even before we take into consideration their other advantages.

2. They will be cheaper to make.

To date, the most significant problem for Team Nuclear has stemmed from the costs associated with gaining approval from the government and then constructing massive plants. Part of the former was and is a matter of overcoming the myths about Team Nuclear's supposed lack of safety, and part of the latter was and is associated with the idea that you have to build every large nuclear plant to somewhat different and detailed technologies and standards. This means a new design for each project, and a new set of materials and logistics to get the plant built. With all of these legislative, logistic, and even physical hoops to jump through, nuclear plants cost a whole lot to build.

Here it is in a nutshell: "While commercial scale reactors... could cost at least $8 billion, DOE officials have projected the first SMRs will cost approximately $1 billion," and can be funded by private enterprise instead of requiring a government loan or subsidy.[16] So we're looking at a substantial reduction in cost right out of the gate, and that's without even considering that SMRs can be created in production-line fashion.

** Some would suggest that the process of building a plant and/or storing its waste leads to the release of greenhouse gases into the atmosphere. Fine, but that same construction process applies to literally all types of electricity-producing plants one could build, including "zero-emission" wind and solar farms. Citing greenhouse gases associated with plant construction as if nuclear power were the only electricity producer subject to this problem is more than a little misleading. What matters to the discussion is not whether greenhouse gases are emitted during construction of the plant; it's whether greenhouse gases are emitted as a result of the process the plant uses to produce electricity.

Why is the production-line potential so important? You recall the story of Henry Ford and how his production-line model made Ford Motors a household name. Well, let's apply those same principles to an SMR. Imagine a scenario in which a single manufacturing plant could churn out a number of identically built nuclear reactors in a short amount of time. Picture reactor after reactor rolling off the production floor like so many Model Ts. It is difficult to overstate just how much of an advantage this could be for Team Nuclear.

For one thing, production-line SMRs would completely eliminate the recurring cost of creating a design for each new nuclear plant. Those designs would already exist and would be put into action every day on the production line. With those designs in hand, once the Nuclear Regulatory Commission approved the basic template, other reactors produced using that same template would have automatic approval.

Before you dismiss this assembly line concept as science fiction, keep in mind that the United States is currently building smaller, land-based reactors, and many of those same kinds of reactors are already operational in other countries. In fact, at the time of this writing, there are 131 smaller reactors (somewhat like the ones you find in a submarine) operating in twenty-six countries.[17] In addition, various countries have developed many new designs for SMRs, with two operational, three under construction, twelve ready for construction, and eight more in earlier stages of planning. A few countries even have SMRs ready to export, the market for which will be enormous.

There is good reason for this growing demand for smaller nuclear reactors: an SMR just makes sense from a size perspective. The smallest SMRs can serve twenty thousand people, and the largest single SMRs would serve approximately three hundred thousand people.[18] Now, that's not quite the size of a large nuclear plant, which can serve upwards of three million people, but it does take care of the problem where many areas of the world can't sustain the sheer size and power output of a large plant. In fact, about 18% of the world's population (approximately 1.3 billion people)[19] lives in areas where large nuclear plants would overload the electrical grid and produce more electricity than needed.[20]

Remember also that SMRs are *modular.* In places where running massive power grids isn't feasible, a single SMR can serve hundreds of thousands of people. In major cities where there isn't room for a large-scale plant, the modular nature of SMRs will allow planners to serve anywhere from hundreds of thousands to millions of customers, depending on the number of SMRs used.

This is where the *modular* part of the name *small modular reactor* becomes so powerful. Yes, it is true that each reactor serves a smaller number of people, but it's also true that you can lay these things side by side and string them together. As small as they are, you could serve as few or as many customers as you needed to. It's all just a matter of ordering up the right number of reactors. If you're serving a small village in Zimbabwe, one reactor will probably suffice. If you're serving one of the five boroughs of New York City, well, you're going to need a few.

The best part? As anyone who has owned modular furniture can tell you, adaptability—namely *expandability*—is an attractive feature. If ever you found your customer base growing to the point at which your existing SMR or network of SMRs couldn't serve them fully, it would just be a matter of ordering a new reactor off the production line and installing it alongside the other(s).

With their lower cost of production, their assembly-line construction potential, and their greater flexibility to serve a variety of populations, whether large or small, SMRs could be providing electricity to as many as one hundred million people by 2040.[21] One hundred million new people with electricity would represent one of the largest advances ever in the global standard of living.

3. They are transportable overseas.

You'll recall the image of an SMR on the back of a semi-truck. Well, those little guys fit onto trains and into transatlantic shipping crates as well. A large part of the beauty of the SMR's compact size is that it makes it possible (and rather easy) to ship them overseas.[22]

If you want to produce electricity, but particularly the kind that is clean in accordance with green initiatives, you usually need a ton of expensive power lines to create a grid to meet the end users' needs. It is difficult and often financially impossible to extend those grids to isolated communities. This is not the case for an SMR, which can be placed near the area where electricity is needed. That is a powerful advantage for Team Nuclear.

"Small modular reactors could serve as 'starter reactors' for countries that have no nuclear power now, no budget for a standard behemoth-size model, and grids too weak to tolerate one anyway."[23] With its portability, diminutive size, and the small amount of land required, an SMR could deliver power to those isolated communities without the need for investment in sophisticated and intricate grids.

An SMR can be placed in virtually any location in the world. There are no communities too remote for it to serve.

The electric grid infrastructure in many parts of the world is unable to support the deployment of large nuclear power plants. Deployed systems must be appropriate to the scale of the national electric grid and other institutional capabilities. For example, building large nuclear plants assumes the presence of an appropriately scaled electric grid infrastructure. If this infrastructure is not present, and it is not in many developing countries, then different technologies are needed, namely, grid-appropriate (modular) nuclear reactors.[24]

But why would we want to give our nuclear reactor technology to other countries? you might ask. First, doing this would not lead to the kind of nuclear proliferation that might have you worried. A nuclear reactor and a nuclear bomb are not even close to the same thing. By sending a developing country a nuclear reactor, we would not be sending them a nuclear weapon, or even the ability to produce one. This is because any purchase agreement for a nuclear reactor would require the country in question to purchase their uranium already sufficiently enriched to fuel a nuclear power plant. They would not be allowed to have the means to enrich it further, to the point where they could make a nuclear bomb.

The real development we would see from a geopolitical perspective would not be increased nuclear tension, but rather a wave of nuclear peace. Why? Because imagine what would happen if you gave the 1.5 billion people currently without access to electricity a reliable, affordable, and entirely clean source of electricity.[25] Then imagine what would happen if you offered a simpler and more effective means to cook and heat a home to the 3 billion people who still use wood and coal to meet those tasks.[26] It would make somewhere between 1.5 and 3 billion more people exponentially more comfortable, which would result in a larger percentage of the world population feeling a little less tense about what they have or do not have.

And now, yes, let's talk about the economic gains. What's the first and best way to get out of a recession? Growth. If the development of countries like China and India tell us anything, then we know that making an electrical grid more sophisticated often follows with an increase in consumer spending. If we're giving 1.5 to 3 billion people living in the developing world greater access to clean and affordable electricity to develop their economies, the growth potential for exports could be nearly overwhelming. Additionally, all that newfound productivity they would enjoy from SMR-produced electricity would allow them to explore the world of additional luxuries that electricity opens up for them. This means 1.5 to 3 billion new people looking to buy goods that would not have been available to them before. The economic boom would be enormous.

4. SMRs can be buried underground.

The other legislative hurdle for Team Nuclear's large plants to clear has always been "Where in the world do we put this big, ugly nuclear plant without angering my constituents?" SMRs like the one on the truck render that discussion irrelevant as well. These babies are so small; you no longer have to worry about constructing massive cooling towers and occupying sprawling spaces. You can bury the reactor underground, as seen in the pictures below.

Small Modular Reactor

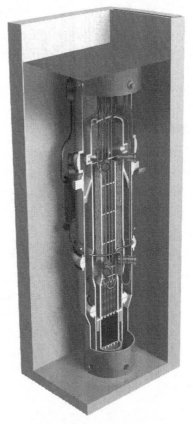

(66' TALL x 12' WIDE)   ...

... A Small Modular Reactor of this size can provide electricity for about 50,000 homes.

Small Modular Reactor Placed Underground

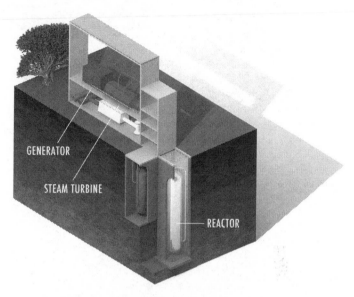

GENERATOR

STEAM TURBINE

REACTOR

Given that they reside entirely underground, the reactors depicted above are completely out of view for anyone walking past. For this kind of plant, the only components that appear *above* ground are those that take the steam created by the reactor and convert it to electricity. The result is not only less surface area that needs to be dedicated to the plant itself, but a more aesthetically pleasing structure as well. Recall that earlier image of the huge cooling towers and above-ground containment structures. Contrasted to that eyesore, here is what a typical SMR plant would look like:

Above Ground Facility with Two Small Modular Reactors

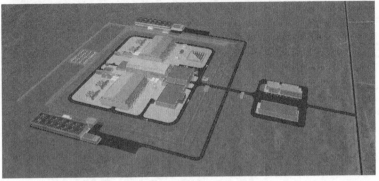

Beyond the obvious safety bonuses (which I'll discuss in the next section), the above picture gives you an idea of how great it is to be able to literally bury your electricity operation in the earth. First, you don't have to worry quite as much about acquiring huge swaths of land (as you would if you were building a wind or solar farm, for example). Second, the next time you drive by a nuclear plant, you won't even know it's there. As you can see above, SMR plants will still require some office space above ground for administrative and maintenance purposes, but the bulk of the actual electricity-producing structure will be out of sight and out of mind for the general public. An SMR-powered nuclear plant would look very similar to any other office complex. No more massive cooling towers.

5. They are safe.

In the next couple of chapters, I'm going to dispel the myths that nuclear power is any less safe than the safest other methods of producing electricity—and the most important one I'm going to address is the myth that nuclear plant reactors can explode like a nuclear bomb (quick spoiler: thanks to some basic laws of physics that I'll get into later, they cannot). For now, keep in mind that the question of safety with SMRs essentially starts and ends with this factor:

In addition to being small enough to ship, the reactors are small enough to be installed underground, offering the advantage of earthquake protection; buried structures are less vulnerable than those above the surface.[27]

Digging deeper,

> This cooling system...relies more on the natural circulation of the cooling medium within the reactor's containment flask than on pumps. This passive cooling is one of the ways that SMRs can improve safety...Since they are smaller and use less fuel, they are easier to cool effectively, which greatly reduces the likelihood of a catastrophic accident or meltdown in the first place...It also eliminates the possibility of one of the frightening episodes of the Fukushima accident where the water in the containment vessel broke down into hydrogen and oxygen and then exploded.
>
> Another advantage of modular design is that some SMRs are small enough to be installed below ground...Underground installations make modular reactors easier to secure and install in a much smaller footprint...Underground installation also enhances security with fewer sophisticated systems needed, which also helps bring down costs. [28]

6. They are completely adaptable.

Setting aside the modular nature of semi-truck-size SMRs for a moment, let's talk about further adaptability thanks to the fact that these things don't even have to be *that* large. Imagine a nuclear reactor the size of a hot tub. This concept is not science fiction.

"A handful of companies are promoting pocket nukes. One startup company, Hyperion Power, touts a 'hot-tub'-size... reactor for about $25 million that could be transported to a site, buried underground, and used to power 20,000 homes."[29] Further reduction in scale could lead to individual companies powering their electricity needs with nuclear plants the size of engines or even refrigerators—and again, all of these reactors are modular and therefore expandable as needs increase.[30]

So imagine a world where developing nations can have access to cheap and clean nuclear power; where every community, no matter how rural, can find electricity from this same source; where any company wishing to unplug from the grid can invest in an in-house nuclear reactor; and where military installations the world over can go green with their own portable nuclear plants. This world exists— and it exists right now. In fact, if you recall our discussion about the 700 ships that have been powered by small nuclear reactors since 1950, you can see that this world has existed for over sixty years. We just haven't embraced the true potential for this technology until now.

One final point about the value of an SMR's adaptability: it makes the SMR particularly appropriate to aid the United States and other countries in their efforts to replace dirty-burning coal plants with greener technologies. Why build an enormous wind farm adjacent to a decommissioned and abandoned coal plant when "these new reactors—smaller than a rail car and one-tenth the cost of a big plant—could be built quickly and... replace existing coal-fired plants that do not meet current federal air quality emission standards"?[31]

With SMRs, we're looking at a clean, cheap, bury-able, transportable, adaptable, and safe source of electricity readily available to anyone willing to make the investment. So when can we start? The latest projections suggest that these may be ready to roll out en masse as early as 2017. The primary barrier at the moment is governmental approval, but as I pointed out, the assembly-line nature of this product will ensure that approval only has to occur once.

The good news for SMRs is that federal loan guarantees worth up to $12.5 billion to support advanced nuclear energy projects recently became a reality. So did an additional $452 million from the Department of Energy to speed up the design and licensing for SMRs.[32]

If we look back at some similar advancements in technology, we can see that SMRs and Team Nuclear in general boast an exciting future. Nuclear development is a little like medical technology and quite a lot like computers. Think about how rapidly emerging technologies in both fields have changed the world. In the realm of electricity production, Team Nuclear and SMRs could make the same kind of impact. The potential for improvement in safety, cost, fuel use, transmission-line requirements, and more, is virtually limitless.

What we are looking at in Team Nuclear is a source of reliable, steady electricity generated on a small piece of land, close to the area that needs the electricity, with inexhaustible, low-cost fuel. It is completely safe because it requires no human action to operate or shut down, it generates little waste (and its waste can be stored safely or recycled into new fuel), is invulnerable to terrorist attack or fuel-stealing, is impervious to destructive acts of nature, can be buried underground, and can do all of this while creating no greenhouse gases or particulate air pollution. On top of that, the technology has only reached about 20% of its potential efficiency. Beat that.

It is not a question of whether all this is possible; it is a question of how quickly the public and politicians can be educated, and how quickly those same politicians can make decisions in favor of nuclear power. It is clear that moving rapidly to increase the percentage of electricity produced by Team Nuclear would be the most effective and efficient way to meet US and world clean electricity needs. It is also the best and most effective way to reduce greenhouse gas. When one considers the important role of government in facilitating increased use of nuclear power, it seems like a waste of government effort and funds to support any team in the Electricity Conference not named Team Nuclear.

But just in case you need more convincing before you jump on the nuclear bandwagon, let's go into a little more depth on the technology behind nuclear power.

Nuclear in Depth

The intent of this chapter is to dispel some of the misconceptions about nuclear power and to explain the environmental, political, and economic potential that the future holds for Team Nuclear. If we want to see that potential in action, then the best place to start is by taking a look at what an ideal nuclear-driven grid looks like. To do this, we have to go abroad.

There is no question about it; the best Team Nuclear in the world currently resides in France. 80% of the country's electricity comes from nuclear power.[1] Their latest-generation nuclear plants are so efficient; they actually *export* electricity to surrounding countries.[2]

The French population and government have consistently supported the use of nuclear power because it provides such low-cost electricity without any particulate pollution or greenhouse gases.[3] The French have moved ahead progressively with sophisticated waste storage techniques as well, and while the country used to store nuclear waste in many secure locations around the country, they are now building a large storage facility far underground, in rocks that haven't moved for a million years.

France is the ideal. But how did it get there? It must be a particularly leftist country, right? Surely they must have a powerful Green movement.

Well, if we cross the border into Germany, we see that a strong Green party isn't the key to nuclear dominance. There, Team Nuclear isn't just weak; it has been *banned from the competition*. This ban is apparently the result of fear over the potential for nuclear disaster, along with the Green party's rather narrow focus on the implications of nuclear waste. This misconception has cost the German people dearly, as they pay substantially higher rates for their electricity than their French neighbors.

> In Germany, renewable-energy subsidies are now costing consumers and industry about $32 billion a year. The costs have become so onerous that...Germany's economy and energy minister Sigmar Gabriel told energy conference attendees in Berlin that his country is risking "dramatic deindustrialization" if it doesn't reduce energy costs. In December, the Center for European Policy Studies, a Brussels-based think tank, reported that European steelmakers are paying twice as much for electricity... as their US competitors. In Denmark, that wonderland for wind-energy enthusiasts, residential electricity now costs...more than three times the US average rate.[4]

The outlook is only going to get worse. If the Green party in Germany succeeds in banning coal, natural gas, and nuclear (as is their stated goal), then in that country, soon it won't be necessary to launch any public service campaigns about turning off light switches to combat global warming, because turning them *on* won't bring any light anyway.

So if it's not a strong Green party that leads to effective clean energy policy, what does it take to become more like France? One of the reasons we don't have more nuclear power in the United States is that many people are afraid it's too dangerous. The average person demonstrates an enormously flawed view regarding the safety of US nuclear facilities. The media and such knowledgeable people as movie stars consistently hyperventilate against nuclear power and as a result have loaded up the antinuclear bandwagon. Yet there is little reporting of the facts with regard to the safety of modern, responsible, and well-regulated nuclear plants like the ones found in the United States and France.

Why is that? Well, it all boils down to fear.

Dispelling the Fear

I can't say I blame most people for harboring negative thoughts about nuclear power. No matter how much nuclear proponents champion its safety, memories of past problems will linger. It's part of the human condition to dwell on the horrors of the past. Strangely, though, when we look at the Electricity Conference, that part of the human condition only seems to apply to Team Nuclear. Despite the fact that we can attribute a monumentally larger number of deaths to fossil fuels, Team Nuclear remains the bad guy in terms of safety.

If we can say it's human nature to remember disasters and ignore prolonged dangers, then why doesn't anyone seem to remember all those disasters we can attribute to Team Water? In 1975, a dam broke in China, killing 171,000 people and rendering another 11 million people homeless. In addition to this catastrophe, the world has seen 30 dam failures that killed a combined total of 7,699 people—and that's just since 1969. If we look solely at the US during that timeframe, eight dams have broken, killing a total of 464 people.[5]

You might be wondering why I chose 1969 as my cutoff date. It's because 1969 was the same year the US installed its first nuclear power plant. Since then, not one member of the public in the United States has died due to the use of nuclear power—not one; zero, zip, none.[6]

Meanwhile, the BP oil disaster of 2010 dominated the American conversation for nearly a year, and yet people seem to have gotten over it already. Collapsed mines, coal plant explosions, and the thousands upon thousands of annual deaths connected to coal plant pollution have done little to shift most of the world's major economic powers from coal mining.

So what gives? Why does nearly every other team in the conference get a pass for their history of death and disaster, but Team Nuclear gets branded as unsafe? Mostly, we owe these disparities to the news media. The reason we hold Team Nuclear to such a different standard is that the two disasters and one nondisaster scattered loosely over the history of nuclear power production were sensational news stories. Nothing sells newspaper copy—or sears itself into a national consciousness—quite like a manmade disaster. In many cases (again, with the exception of dam breakages, for some reason), manmade disasters can come to brand a technology as unsafe or unfeasible. Nuclear power seems to carry that brand despite a history of total safety in the United States (including at Three Mile Island), and despite recent dramatic improvements to safety around the world.

I mentioned Three Mile Island, so we should probably discuss it. Well, that's the nondisaster I mentioned just above. The media put in an excellent effort at making it *look* like a disaster, but in fact, Three Mile Island is the perfect example of a safety system that worked *precisely as designed*. "With proper perspective, Three Mile Island can (and should) be characterized as a shining example of how well the safety systems work, even in the face of human error and old-fashioned reactor design."[7]

What the media wanted people to believe following the incident at Three Mile Island is this: thousands were doomed to cancer because of a major mistake at an American nuclear facility.

What actually happened was this: a valve broke, causing coolant to leak into the containment unit of the reactor. The loss of coolant raised the temperature of the core, which led to a partial meltdown of the reactor. Even though the instrumentation faltered, hampering workers' ability to respond, and even though the people in charge of containing the problem made their best efforts to bungle it completely, the containment structure *worked as designed*.

The result of this supposed catastrophe? Zero deaths or injuries. This is because the 25,000 people who lived within five miles of the plant were exposed to radiation no worse than a chest X-ray.[8] By the way, an X-ray is equivalent to 2.4 days' worth of the natural radiation you receive every day just by living on Earth, which is nowhere near the ballpark of the level of radiation necessary to cause physical harm.[9]

In summary, the only thing that happened at Three Mile Island in 1979 was that a nuclear containment structure did its job, totally and completely.

Of course, Three Mile Island isn't the only incident we can point to from Team Nuclear's past. Opponents are always quick to point to Chernobyl as evidence that this technology just isn't safe enough. Chernobyl was indeed the first of only two true nuclear plant disasters in world history. The story of how it occurred starts with the sterile-sounding word *containment*. When we're talking about a nuclear plant, what does containment mean? Containment refers to the concrete and steel structure designed to encase the reactor and prevent unintentional emissions. A nuclear reaction is a volatile phenomenon. An adequate containment structure will prevent any adverse emissions from reaching the environment.

Here is what an adequate containment structure looks like:

Container Building Surrounding Large Nuclear Reactor

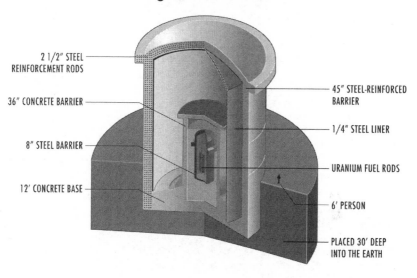

2 1/2" STEEL REINFORCEMENT RODS

36" CONCRETE BARRIER

8" STEEL BARRIER

12' CONCRETE BASE

45" STEEL-REINFORCED BARRIER

1/4" STEEL LINER

URANIUM FUEL RODS

6' PERSON

PLACED 30' DEEP INTO THE EARTH

The above depicts a plant put in operation by the Nuclear Energy Institute. While not all containment structures in the US are exactly the same in every detail, they must all meet government standards for containing radioactivity and preventing it from reaching the environment even under severely adverse conditions. In this case, the first barrier is the external enclosure wall you see in the picture above. That's 45 inches of concrete reinforced by four 2.5-inch steel rods embedded vertically and horizontally one foot apart throughout the barrier. The second barrier is a 36-inch concrete enclosure around the reactor. The last barrier is an 8-inch steel casing molded around the reactor. The bottom of the reactor is 12 feet of solid concrete. In addition, the entire containment structure is placed into hard-packed ground.[10]

The government standard for these containment structures, as enforced by the Nuclear Regulatory Commission, is that the structure must be strong enough to withstand impact from the world's largest airplane fully loaded with fuel and people. Think of the planes that crashed into and destroyed the World Trade Center. The containment structure of a nuclear plant is mandated to be strong enough to withstand that kind of blow.

For further context, consider the nuclear plant in the southern US that happened to be directly in the path of one of the deadliest hurricanes in US history, Hurricane Andrew in August of 1992. The storm did 90 million dollars' worth of damage to the buildings surrounding the containment structure, but the containment structure itself was undamaged.[11]

Large Nuclear Reactor

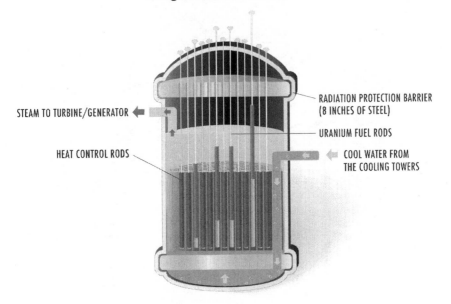

STEAM TO TURBINE/GENERATOR ⬅

RADIATION PROTECTION BARRIER
(8 INCHES OF STEEL)

URANIUM FUEL RODS

HEAT CONTROL RODS

COOL WATER FROM
THE COOLING TOWERS ⬅

The containment structure is only part of the array of safety measures we find in a modern nuclear plant. Above is a schematic of a large nuclear reactor. While reactors vary in size, an average one is 45 feet tall (about the same height as a four-story building) and 20 feet wide.

As you can see from the image above, the way it works is easy to understand: cool water enters the containment structure from the cooling tower. There, the nuclear fuel rods heat the water until it produces steam. The steam then activates a turbine in a generator that creates electricity. The hot water from the condensed steam then flows into the cooling towers, where it is cooled and then recycled back into the containment structure, where the process repeats itself.

So we know how a containment structure works, but how does the actual nuclear reaction work? It all starts with Einstein's famous equation $E=MC^2$.

That equation states that "energy equals mass times the speed of light squared." This means that, when a very small amount of mass is destroyed, it results in a huge amount of energy.[12] That's exactly what we're trying to do when we create a nuclear reaction. In the United States, we create that nuclear reaction through the use of uranium. Naturally occurring uranium exists in a form we call U-238, but naturally occurring uranium cannot fuel a nuclear reactor. Before we can create a nuclear reaction, a certain percentage of the uranium we're using has to be enriched. The enriched version we call U-235. It is U-235, and not U-238, that is capable of generating the chain reaction that creates heat, and in turn, electricity.

In the case of uranium, when a neutron pierces a U-235 atom, the atom ejects two neutrons, each of which pierces another U-235 atom, resulting in the ejection of four more neutrons, and so on in a chain reaction where minuscule parts of matter are transformed into energy as per Einstein's equation. This chain reaction produces heat. Lots of it. That heat is sent through a sophisticated system that produces steam to rotate turbines just like those found in a gas- or coal-fired plant, ultimately producing the stuff that turns on your lights.

The distinction between U-238 and U-235 is also the reason why, despite what nuclear opponents might have led you to believe, it is absolutely impossible for a nuclear plant to explode like a bomb. There is simply not enough of the volatile U-235 present in a nuclear reactor to create the kind of chain reaction that leads to an explosion. For a nuclear bomb, you need a whole lot more U-235 than you'll find in a nuclear reactor. A bomb requires a minimum of 90% U-235 to 10% U-238. A nuclear plant is the reverse: 90% U-238 and 10% U-235. To create a nuclear bomb from uranium, you have to enrich a lot of uranium to a high enough percentage of U-235, which is an extraordinarily difficult and costly process. So take solace in the notion that your nearest nuclear plant *can't be* a ticking time bomb.

But what does it look like when a containment structure doesn't measure up to US standards? On April 26, 1986, one of four operational nuclear reactors at Chernobyl in the Soviet Union suffered a major disaster. Before we get into the question of how, let's reiterate an important point: there are no nuclear reactors in the United States (or anywhere else in the world) that are like the faulty reactor at Chernobyl. For one thing, "All the Chernobyl reactors were… water-cooled, graphite-moderated—a design that American

GARY SCHWENDIMAN

physicist and Nobel laureate Hans Bethe has called 'fundamentally faulty, having a built-in instability.'"[13] For another, Chernobyl's reactors didn't have a containment structure like the one I just described above. Rather than enjoying the containment of many feet and layers of steel-reinforced concrete, the reactors at Chernobyl were covered by a light concrete shell. Since then, important changes have been made in all Soviet Union-designed reactors. As a result, "A repetition of the 1986 Chernobyl accident is now virtually impossible."[14]

You might think that such a woefully insufficient barrier was what did in the Chernobyl reactor, but you would be wrong. "Without question, the accident at Chernobyl was the result of a fatal combination of ignorance and complacency. 'As members of a select scientific panel convened immediately after the... accident,' writes Bethe, 'my colleagues and I established that the Chernobyl disaster tells us about the deficiencies of the Soviet political and administrative system rather than about problems with nuclear power.'"[15]

I love that quotation. I can't imagine a better way to sum up what happened in April 1986 than as an indictment of the inherent flaws in the system that governed the people working that day. The main problem wasn't the substandard containment structure or faulty design of the reactor, although those issues certainly contributed. It was really a problem of incompetence and the special kind of management that results from Communism. Under Communism, the buck doesn't stop anywhere. Everyone gets paid pretty much the same, regardless of quality of work or role, so no one has an incentive to assume responsibility. For anything. Hence, when something awful happens, you don't see too many people charging forward to take responsibility.

The Chernobyl accident happened in part because the people on staff during the day shift were anxious to perform a test of one of the plant's safety systems. The irony is thick here. The worst nuclear disaster in history occurred because somebody got careless with a safety test. Right when the test was about to happen, the regional grid manager from Kiev called to say that one of the plants in the grid had to go down, so Chernobyl would need to stay at full production. It wasn't until the night shift came on that they finally got the green light to run the safety test. By then, it was way past the deadline to get it done, so the lead decision maker—still a novice at his job, all things considered—pushed the system to the brink. In response to the pressure of the situation, he made a series of rash decisions that, in retrospect, appear to have been motivated more by the desire to get the test finished quickly than by the desire to avoid the disaster with which he was flirting.[16]

Some of the people on staff that day were only part-timers. Some were retired miners. Some were firefighters who knew nothing about radiation. Well-established limits on what may and may not be done with an unstable reactor were ignored. The faulty design of the control rods actually *accelerated* the reaction rather than reducing it. The conglomeration of errors led to a reaction that went out of control, ultimately sparking through the completely inadequate concrete shell and turning Chernobyl and the area many miles around it into an uninhabitable wasteland.

There is a rather broad range in the number of reported deaths related or potentially related to the Chernobyl disaster. A total of 47 people died from acute radiation syndrome contracted while working at the disaster site,[17] and as many as 16,000 radiation-related cancer deaths may have occurred or will occur as a result of global exposure to the fallout.[18] That latter number may actually wind up being greater or less than 16,000, by the way. The highly reputable World Health Organization puts the total at 4,000 deaths over the long term, while the well-known anti-nuclear group Greenpeace estimates 93,000 deaths. I chose 16,000 deaths because it falls somewhere in the middle of the various estimates, and I don't want to minimize the impact of the disaster. Whatever number you choose, one clear point remains: Chernobyl as a plant certainly had severe flaws built in by human designers, but it also failed almost entirely because of human error on the part of the operators.

As a quick aside, if we can accept that number of 16,000 Chernobyl-related deaths, it should be pointed out that about the same number of deaths occurs every year as a result of the air pollution attributed to coal plants operating in the United States. So "unsafe" nuclear power potentially led to the deaths of 16,000 people worldwide once in its history, but "safer" coal plants kill about that same number of people in the United States alone every single year, and more than three million people per year die worldwide from coal plant pollution.

Next is the Fukushima nuclear accident in Japan, but let's do things in reverse order and first give you the bottom line—a bottom line that will contradict everything you have read, seen, or heard about that incident. The bottom line is this: no one died and no one got sick as a result of the accident. Does that surprise you? The following statement comes from a report commissioned by the United Nations Committee on the Effects of Atomic Radiation (which is a committee of 80 scientists from 18 countries): "The tsunami hit a nuclear plant built to a 50-year-old design and *no one died*."[19] The emphasis on that last phrase is mine. Also, "No radiation-related deaths or acute effects have been observed among the workers involved at the accident site."[20] And finally, "...the residents of the area who were evacuated were exposed to so little radiation that radiation-induced health impacts are likely to be below detectable levels."[21]

Don't get me wrong; I acknowledge that the accident in question was a huge disaster. It destroyed the plant, forced the relocation of thousands of people, resulted in the closure of all the other 54 Japanese nuclear plants for at least two years, and set back plans for the building of many safe, efficient, non-greenhouse-gas-producing nuclear plants worldwide. All I'm saying here is that there were zero human deaths as a result of the accident.

The Fukushima nuclear plant disaster clearly resulted from incompetent planning and leadership. Of course, it didn't help that it was sparked by a disastrous natural phenomenon of historic proportions, but the fact remains that avoidable human mistakes were made. For example, the Japanese knew that tsunamis had occurred twice along the same coastline in Japanese history.[22] That fact was ignored when the plant location was chosen.

Without doubt, the primary issue was that the Japanese government and the company that managed the Fukushima plant were just plain overconfident about matters of safety.[23] But let's not lump the blame on the people in charge just yet. Let's examine the facts at hand before we draw any conclusions.

First, we know that a 45-foot tsunami rocked the coast of Japan in March 2011. That tsunami killed more than 19,000 people while disabling the power supply and cooling systems of three of the reactors at Fukushima. All three of the reactor cores melted down almost completely. While the reported amount of total radiation released after the first few days varies greatly depending on whether you are reading a Japanese or non-Japanese news source, it is clear that there was some radiation released (although, as I mentioned, it wasn't enough to do any real harm).

So did the containment structure of the plant work, preventing radiation from escaping? Well, yes and no. One thing we do know for certain is that the containment facilities held up well against the quake. The problem was that they could not withstand the tsunami—or, more accurately, the measures put in place did not properly consider what might happen in the event of a tsunami.

When things start to go wrong in a nuclear plant, it's because there is too much out-of-control heat. This is usually the result of the water-cooling system not working properly. If you don't have water to cool the reaction, then it just gets hotter and hotter, creating radioactive gas that eventually generates enormous pressure. What happened at Fukushima was that the tsunami knocked out the electricity, so the cooling pumps quit working. The plant did have backup generators in place, as almost all nuclear plants do, to help avert such an occurrence. These were big diesel generators that could provide electricity to pump the cooling water for days and days without issue. The problem was that the generators were installed in the *basement*, which exposed them to the flood created by the tsunami.

That isn't the full story of Fukushima, however. There was a cultural component as well. Even the Japanese investigatory commission took the people running the plant to task for adhering to Japanese cultural quirks rather than building the plant correctly. According to the Japanese investigatory commission's chairman, Fukushima's "fundamental causes are to be found in the ingrained conventions of Japanese culture: our reflexive obedience; our reluctance to question authority; our devotion to 'sticking with the program'; our groupism; and our insularity."[24] Even though the company responsible for the reactors was aware of the potential that the backup generators would be disabled in the event of a flood, they did nothing about it. Instead, they went around telling each other that there was no need to prepare for the possibility of severe flooding. As a result, the first responders to the flood weren't trained on how to resolve the issue and were thus woefully unprepared to control the accident.

In summary, the second-worst disaster in the history of nuclear power occurred because of a historically large tsunami, some boneheaded positioning of backup generators, a refusal by high-level managers to listen to employees, the bureaucratic nature of corporate communication within the Japanese culture, and an administrative refusal to change "the program" to avoid disaster that a ruling body actually saw coming five years in advance.

Out of 438 nuclear plants in operation worldwide,[25] only two actual disasters have occurred in the over half-century of nuclear power. In other words, a nuclear plant, well constructed, positioned, and managed, isn't anywhere near as dangerous as you may have thought. Even with this incredible track record of success, nuclear plants continue to improve in terms of safety every year.

Uranium at a Glance

Let's move on to another common misconception about nuclear energy: that the stuff you need to make it work isn't plentiful enough to make investment in the technology worthwhile. This idea is, in a word, misguided. The truth is that uranium is a common element. You find it in rocks and seawater.[26] Try to imagine the sheer number of rocks and amount of seawater on the planet. Depending on what data you're examining, there's really quite a lot of uranium for the taking—enough to power the world's electricity needs for tens or even hundreds of thousands of years, by some estimates.[27]

So uranium is plentiful. But in which countries' territories do you find it? Well, there's good news on this front. Unlike with gasoline, we find it chiefly within the borders of our political allies. So when we're thinking about gathering uranium, are we facing the possibility of another OPEC-type situation in which the supplier dictates the market price and holds global stability in the palm of its hand? In a word: no.* Not unless you're threatened by the instability of places like Australia and Canada. Fortunately for Team Nuclear, there is an abundance of uranium in politically stable and friendly countries. In fact, 24% of the world's uranium can be found in Australia. Another 9% resides in Canada.

Okay fine. We can trade with US-friendly countries. But how much does it cost? And do those costs make the investment in nuclear power reasonable? Let's take a look.

When we're talking about nonrenewable electricity sources, Team Nuclear's primary competition is from coal and natural gas. The problem coal and natural gas face is that their plants are sensitive to the cost of the

---

* Even though the United States imports some uranium, it could provide enough of its own uranium at a slightly higher cost than by importing it, thus eliminating the need to import it and maintaining full electricity independence.

fuel used to run them. A comparatively large percentage of the total cost to run a coal or natural gas plant is attributable to the cost of the fuel.

Team Nuclear doesn't suffer from the same issue because you need so much less uranium to run a nuclear plant than you would need fuel to run a coal plant or a natural gas plant. For coal and natural gas, fuel makes up 80% of a plant's operating costs. By contrast, for a nuclear plant, the cost of the fuel represents only 30% of the overall operating costs,** which means that the operating cost for a nuclear plant is practically immune to fluctuations in the price of uranium.[28]

The next time you hear the story about how there's not enough uranium to last us more than a couple hundred years, and that the relative lack of uranium will lead to exorbitantly high prices for nuclear power, don't believe the hype. There is a nearly infinite supply of uranium in the world, so it's relatively cheap.

Oh, also, it's not the only potential fuel for a nuclear reactor. In fact, it's not even the most plentiful potential fuel for a nuclear reactor. Thorium is.

Thorium at a Glance

Thorium is the 90th element in the periodic table (uranium is the 92nd). Named for the Norse thunder god Thor, thorium is found at low levels in rock, soil, and water, and thus in plants and animals. It is radioactive in all its forms.[29] Thorium in its natural form (as a rock-like substance) can't be used as a fuel for a nuclear reactor. Rather, it has to undergo a complicated process to be transformed into a special isotope, much as U-238 must be enriched into U-235. To make reading of this section easier, we're just going to refer to the fuel as "thorium" instead of laboriously naming the specialized isotope of thorium that runs a nuclear reactor.[30]

The important part, in any case, is that thorium has many potential advantages over uranium and appears to be another advantage for Team Nuclear over the rest of the Electricity Conference. In fact, for those concerned about the myths that uranium-fueled nuclear plants are unsafe, cause possible nuclear proliferation, may lead to theft of uranium by terrorists

---

** Half of that 30% is the cost of enriching the uranium and making fuel pellets for the fuel rods.

planning to make bombs, that the use of uranium creates massive amounts of dangerous nuclear waste, or even that the world may run out of uranium, I have good news for you: thorium is so abundant and safe that it doesn't get accused of those things, even by people who are fanatically opposed to nuclear power.

Today, the number of proponents—including top scientists, government officials, and informed citizens—who favor using thorium to fuel nuclear power plants is increasing in the US and worldwide.[31] These proponents generally assert that thorium has the following advantages over uranium:

Advantage: A uranium reactor requires complex safety systems to ensure that the reaction always remains contained, while for a thorium reactor, passive safety is built right in. The way a uranium reactor works is like this: pellets of uranium are stacked into rods that are placed next to control rods, which can slow down or stop the nuclear reaction to reduce heat when necessary. When the nuclear reaction occurs, this heats the rods, which in turn causes the water to turn into steam. The steam is piped to a turbine that turns a generator, which creates electricity.

Thorium-fueled nuclear plants, however, can use an entirely different setup called a "molten salt reactor." It works like this: small thorium pellets get placed in a closed circular containment vessel that contains a slurry of liquid salt. The salt slurry heats up from the thorium reaction. A heat exchanger extracts this heat and turns it into the steam that rotates the turbine. The cooled molten salt circulates until it is hot again. Why is this important? Because it means that the liquid thorium fuel in a molten salt reactor cannot "melt down" like uranium pellets in a rod. If ever a thorium plant encountered a loss of power or overheating in its reactor, the salt in the slurry would automatically dissolve a plug that would release the fuel into a cooling tank underneath.[32] Just like with the passive safety systems we discussed previously, a molten salt reactor doesn't require human intervention because it allows physics to do all the safety work.[33] This makes a thorium-fueled nuclear plant even safer than any of the plants previously discussed, which is in turn a further advantage for Team Nuclear.

Advantage: Using thorium to fuel nuclear power does not result in the possibility of creating nuclear weapons. At the time of this writing, we see worldwide pressure to reduce the threat of countries enriching uranium beyond what is necessary for nuclear power plants in order to make bombs.

Iran makes plenty of headlines with its claim that it intends to use its enrichment facilities solely for the purposes of nuclear power and not for nuclear weapons. With thorium, the problem becomes irrelevant because thorium, for all practical purposes, cannot be enriched and therefore can't be used to make a nuclear weapon.[34] Thus, anyone opposed to nuclear power solely because of the notion that it could lead to the proliferation of nuclear weapons should enjoy the potential in using thorium as a nuclear fuel.

Advantage: It is terrorism-proof. For anyone *still* concerned about what might happen with thorium nuclear fuel if it fell into the hands of a terrorist, take heart: the thorium isotope that can be used for nuclear fuel actually emits lethal gamma rays.[35] So stealing thorium fuel would be so dangerous that no one would be dumb enough to try it.

Advantage: Less waste. Thorium-fueled nuclear reactors create much less waste than uranium-fueled reactors. Also, thorium waste deteriorates much faster than the waste from uranium.[36]

Advantage: Far less pressure. Thorium-fueled plants need no pressurization because they work at atmospheric pressure. In a uranium-fueled reactor, the water is under extreme pressure, so the plant needs thick containment structures to prevent problems from occurring. Thorium reactors do not need such extensive (or expensive) protection.[37]

Advantage: It works in nearly every kind of existing reactor. Thorium fuel can be used not just in molten salt reactors, but in the five most commonly built nuclear power plants in the world. In other words, much like with ethanol's ability to quickly and easily replace gasoline at every gas pump in the country, we don't have to change much of anything about the existing nuclear power infrastructure, other than the fuel.[38]

Advantage: It's still a zero-emissions technology. Like uranium-fueled reactors, thorium-fueled reactors produce zero greenhouse gases during operation.

Advantage: There is four times as much thorium in the earth as there is uranium. Several countries possess massive deposits of the element. Australia has 18.7% of the world's thorium. The US has 15.3%. Meanwhile, Turkey has 13.2%, India has 12.2%, Brazil has 11.6%, and Venezuela has 11.5%. These six countries control 82.55% of the discovered thorium deposits in the world.[39]

Advantage: You don't need nearly as much thorium as uranium to fuel a nuclear reactor. According to a prominent Nobel Prize-winning nuclear scientist, just one ton of thorium can produce as much energy as 200 tons of uranium or 3,500,000 tons of coal.[40]

While not everyone agrees with every stitch of the advantages stated above, it is clear that there are enough good reasons to use thorium that it is now being researched worldwide by countries with nuclear power plants. Many nations have active programs with the intent of building thorium-fueled nuclear power plants. The nations currently involved in significant research on using thorium as a nuclear fuel include Brazil, Belgium, China, Canada, France, Germany, India, Japan, the Netherlands, Norway, Russia, the United Kingdom, and the United States.[41]

With the dire need for green electricity, thorium is certainly worth pursuing. There are simply too many benefits to ignore. "The thorium fuel cycle offers enormous energy security benefits in the long term—due to its potential for being a self-sustaining fuel without the need for fast neutron reactors."[42] Further, thorium "is four times as abundant as uranium and as common as lead. The Thorium Energy Alliance (TEA) estimates 'there is enough thorium in the United States alone to power the country at its current energy level for over 1,000 years.'"[43] Perhaps most compellingly, thorium has passive safety built right in. "Meltdown is impossible, since nuclear chain reactions cannot be sustained, and fission stops by default in case of accident."[44] With thorium, it's impossible to have the kind of meltdown that caused the disasters at Fukushima and Chernobyl.

For those concerned about proliferation of nuclear weapons, "It is difficult to make a practical nuclear bomb from a thorium reactor's byproducts."[45] For those concerned about waste, "There is much less nuclear waste—up to two orders of magnitude less… eliminating the need for large-scale or long-term storage. The radioactivity of the resulting waste also drops down to safe levels after just a few hundred years."[46]

If this sounds like a fantasy world, I'm happy to inform you that it isn't. Almost all of the initial research on the use of thorium fuel was conducted in the US. During various stretches between 1950 and 1980, the US had four experimental thorium-fueled plants in operation. With no shortage of electricity in the US, with modern uranium-fueled nuclear plants producing 20% of the nation's electricity, and with a perfect nuclear safety record, the US had little incentive to fund further research on thorium. But when we think about thorium's worldwide implementation, it's clear that the technology's future is bright.

One can get a glimpse of the future for thorium as a fuel by looking at the current developments regarding thorium in India and China, with India ahead but China developing rapidly. Both are miles ahead of the rest of the world in terms of their plans to use thorium and to increase nuclear power generation across the board. This is for good reason: both China and India produce a majority of their electricity from coal and only 3% from nuclear power.[47] These two countries are in a virtual race to see how quickly and effectively they can increase their nuclear power capabilities. Meanwhile, they are both heavily invested in using thorium as a fuel for their new nuclear reactors. Additionally, India is planning to export its new thorium-based technologies around the world. Meanwhile, since the uranium-fueled plants in the US are successful and safe, the US is doing only minimal work on thorium, with one thorium research project expected to be operational in 2015.

Clearly the Indian government sees the benefit in nuclear technology, in part because India is rife with thorium. So motivated are they to get a plant up and running that in late June 2012 they announced their first commercial thorium reactor, which will make India the world leader in production of electricity using thorium.

Team Nuclear versus the Fossil Fuels

Speaking of the competition, let's turn our attention now to an examination of just how Team Nuclear would fare head-to-head against its chief opponents in the Electricity Conference. For these next sections, it is important that we put any safety or economic viability biases aside and just focus on the known qualities each team brings to the table. Doing so will allow us to arrive at the most accurate determination as to which team will emerge victorious.

I would be remiss if I didn't start with Team Coal, given that they have been such a major player in the conference for such a long time. Well, it was a nice run for Team Coal, but as the most polluting technology, it appears dead in the water in this conference. Yes, it is cheap, but given the natural gas boom, along with the dependable low cost of nuclear power, it isn't always the cheapest. It is well established in terms of plant numbers, but those plants are also easily replaced. Many will soon be on their way out, to be replaced by cleaner technologies like small modular reactors.

I mentioned the natural gas boom. This is because there is currently plenty of fervor in the US about fracking and the notion that using natural gas as fuel for the internal combustion engine could finally lead to fuel independence. Ignoring natural gas would be like ignoring the proverbial elephant in the room. Team Natural Gas is surely the team with the hottest buzz behind it at the time of this writing. New technologies are allowing us to tap into much more of the natural gas to be found under the United States than we could previously. This currently abundant natural gas has recently been championed as the answer to many of the country's economic and environmental woes.

I must admit that, in the short term, Team Natural Gas does present a very real threat to the supremacy of Team Nuclear. This is entirely because, with the overwhelming supply of natural gas we're currently seeing on the market, natural gas is cheaper than nuclear power and better for the environment than coal. There is also the illusion of long-term abundance, an illusion that I will address in detail as we discuss natural gas as a replacement for the more dominant fuels in the Fuel Conference. For now, let me just say that there is so much current abundance of natural gas that the United States will eventually start exporting the commodity, which will drastically change its pricing dynamic.

Aside from all that, the supply isn't going to hold where it is currently. This is because, after their first year in operation, shale gas wells (which account for about 40% of natural gas production in the United States), have demonstrated rapid production decline rates. That's just one reason that several experts have called the current boom in natural gas supply a "shale gas bubble." Like other bubbles in history, when it pops, it won't be pretty.[48] It will lead to a reduction in new wells being drilled, which will lead to further production decline, which will of course eventually lead to an increase in natural gas prices.[49]

Once the mechanisms for transporting natural gas (via liquid natural gas, or LNG) around the world to places like Europe and Japan are fully developed, prices will climb further, as natural gas will officially become a globally traded commodity. What will exports of natural gas mean for the world price? Who knows? But what is clear is that, if we have more gas in the United States than we can use, and we wind up exporting it to other countries as a result, it's going to increase the price of gas domestically.

So natural gas has two current advantages over Team Nuclear, and we know that one of them is probably going away. The supply questions, export potential, and price volatility of natural gas make for a shaky long-term investment when compared to the steady costs of nuclear power.

Now to the question of its impact on the environment. Natural gas does cut the particulate-matter impact on the air in half by comparison with Team Coal, but it doesn't have to beat Team Coal on this front. It has to beat Team Nuclear, and Team Nuclear is a net-zero producer of particulate matter. Team Natural Gas, like Team Coal, just can't compete.

Team Nuclear versus Teams Wind and Solar

Since fossil fuels are responsible for much of the greenhouse gases we create worldwide, governmental institutions have put in place certain support mechanisms, including direct subsidies, to increase the amount of electricity produced without causing greenhouse gas release. At present, the government directs many of those subsidies to wind turbines and solar panels.

The problem with this plan is this: wind and solar have the technology to reduce greenhouse gas emission, but whether it's possible to implement enough of them to create a significant impact on greenhouse gas reduction is a matter of some debate. Here's why: to equal the electricity output of one large nuclear reactor, you would need four hundred wind turbines working on 90 square miles of land. And that's if the wind were blowing 100% of the time. Unfortunately for Team Wind, on average, the wind only blows 33% of the time. Therefore, you really need 1,200 wind turbines working on 270 square miles, which is equal to 130,680 football fields.[50] No matter where you stand in the green energy debate, I think we can agree that that's quite a lot of land.

Team Solar has a similar problem. For solar to equal the electricity output of one large nuclear reactor, you would need 11 square miles of solar panels. And that's if the sun were shining 100% of the time. However, on average, the sun only shines enough for solar panels to generate electricity 25% of the time. Therefore, you really need 44 square miles of solar panels, which is equal to 21,296 football fields.[51]

Since technology for wind and solar still has some room for advancement, the land required per unit of output is destined to become less. Even so, one thing remains clear: the land required for this technology compared to the land required for a nuclear plant (particularly of the SMR variety) is enormous. A large nuclear power plant occupies an area of only one to two square miles and can be set up within a reasonable distance from wherever the electricity is consumed. In the case of an SMR supplying electricity for 300,000 people, you only need a piece of land the size of a very large Walmart and its parking lots to get the job done.[52] Additionally, a nuclear plant produces electricity 24 hours a day, all day and all night, regardless of the weather.[53]

Needless to say, for wind and solar, there's just not enough land near densely populated areas. This factor makes the cost and difficulty of transmission for wind and solar much higher than for coal, natural gas, or nuclear. While it is reasonable to project that people will find success with small applications of subsidized solar panels on the roofs of businesses or homes, the chance that solar power will produce large, competitive amounts of electricity over the long run is so low in probability as to be rendered meaningless. So while it is true that Team Solar is currently making progress, much of that progress is because Team Nuclear remains so misunderstood. Once nuclear power receives the attention and understanding it deserves, Team Nuclear's competitive edge over every other team in the conference will become clear.

Team Nuclear Can't Lose

Nuclear power is far safer than you have been led to believe. As an electricity producer, given its vast fuel supply, it has a longer-term viability than we can possibly project. It is a constantly evolving technology with much greater potential for improvement than any other member of the conference. It has already proven itself to be an attractive and completely feasible means of meeting the world's energy needs. In terms of air pollution, it is every bit as green as wind and solar power, and without any of the issues wind and solar suffer from when the wind doesn't blow or the sun doesn't shine. The costs for raw uranium are about one-fifth the cost of fuel for coal and natural gas plants.[54]

These are just few of the reasons that Team Nuclear will be the clear winner of the Electricity Conference and a truly formidable opponent in the Clean Energy Bowl. But for this study to be conclusive, "a few reasons" just aren't enough. No, to show that our champion deserves the crown, we'll need to address all ten.

Just for fun, let's break down those 360 mrems to see if we can figure out which sources of radiation exposure are more "dangerous" than living near a nuclear power plant.* You might just be surprised to learn how close to home some of these are.

We'll get the big ones out the way first: three hundred of the mrems you're exposed to every year come from natural sources.[2] Two hundred of those come directly from the slightly irradiated ground beneath your feet.**

Other entirely natural sources include the masonry in your home. If you live in brick, stone, or adobe, you're enjoying seven mrem per year from the natural radiation in rock. These levels vary depending on how much rock is involved. At Grand Central Station, for instance, where the granite walls contain a great deal of uranium, the exposure for employees is as high as 120 mrem per year.

Also, if you're concerned about overexposure to radiation, instead of moving away from the nuclear plant, you might first think about sleeping alone. Sleeping next to someone for eight hours at night exposes you to two mrem per year. This is because everyone carries around a certain level of potassium in their body, and that potassium is slightly radioactive. Sleep too close to someone, and you're irradiating yourself, albeit at an exceedingly minor level.

How about some of the manmade sources? More bad news, smokers: regular smoking can expose you to as many as 16,000 mrem per year! That's nearly 45 times the baseline rate of exposure. This is because the tobacco in your cigarettes absorbs a large number of elements that are radioactive.

Air travel contributes a millirem for every thousand miles flown. So all you jetsetters out there would do well to stop worrying about nuclear plants and start worrying about what all that flying

---

* And I put "dangerous" in quotes here because, again, living close to a nuclear plant exposes you to one mrem per year, and it takes a dose of 50,000 mrems in a year before we start seeing a potential link to cancer.
** We owe this truth to the very creation of the universe. The Big Bang was such a massively radioactive event that we're still feeling the effects billions of years later.

might be doing to your bodies. (By the way, I don't think you really need to worry—we're still talking tiny doses here.)

Next up are two of my favorites: porcelain teeth/crowns and Brazil nuts. Yes, you read those entries right. While we're dealing with just tenths of a millirem—about on par with the radiation contribution from nuclear plants—your dental work and your nut-eating habit could be upping your exposure to radiation.

Then there's probably the favorite of anyone exasperated with Congress: "[The Capitol] building is so radioactive, due to the high uranium content in its granite walls, it could never be licensed as a nuclear power reactor site."[3]

If there are any congressmen or congresswomen reading this book, first let me apologize for that remark. Then let me implore you to please keep in mind that opponents of Team Nuclear are applying this radiation discussion to the wrong team. The fear really should reside with Team Coal. "The waste produced by coal plants is actually more radioactive than that generated by their nuclear counterparts. In fact, the fly ash emitted by a power plant—a byproduct of burning coal for electricity—carries into the surrounding environment 100 times more radiation than a nuclear power plant producing the same amount of energy."[4]

As a final note, I'll leave a reminder: you have to get all the way up to 50,000 mrem per year before you find a direct correlation between radiation exposure and cancer. So don't worry about that minimal exposure you may be getting from a nearby nuclear plant. It doesn't even begin to scratch the surface of what we can consider dangerous levels.

Okay, now we've put the radiation myth to bed, we can move on to the one about nuclear waste. This is a favorite subject for opponents of Team Nuclear. The misconceptions go like this: nuclear plants create large amounts of radioactive waste (false) that can't be stored without obliterating the environment (false). When this waste accumulates, it has to be transported to unstable storage facilities (false). This of course exposes thousands upon thousands of people to radiation and unacceptable environmental risk during the transport (false). Then, once we do store this stuff, it remains deadly poisonous for an alarming 10,000 years (*very* false).

The truth is that nuclear waste is a much smaller problem than you might think, and the vast majority of it can now be recycled anyway.

Before we dive into the facts, let's define what nuclear waste is, because it's a pretty misunderstood concept. Nuclear waste is nuclear *fuel* that no longer produces enough heat to be useful in a reactor. Today, that waste is stored in one of two ways: either in cement holding ponds near the plant (ponds that immerse the waste in 30 feet of circulating water), or in dry caskets designed to dissipate the heat the waste continues to create. The waste is stored in this way for up to 50 years, by which time it becomes easier and safer to either a) move it to permanent, deep-underground storage or b) recycle it as new fuel that goes back into the plant.[5]

Opponents of Team Nuclear will tell you that nuclear waste is no small issue. In fact, the more vehement among them would have you believe that there's so much of the stuff, we'll be facing nothing short of environmental catastrophe if we don't immediately close down every nuclear plant currently operating on the planet. I have to say, I'm impressed by the sheer outlandishness of that one, because it's not even in the same *stadium* as the truth. In fact, while we're talking about stadiums, let's put this whole matter into football terms. If we somehow managed to collect every ounce of nuclear waste produced over the 50-plus years of nuclear energy in the United States, how many football fields could we fill? Well, we'd be talking about 69,000 tons of the stuff, which sounds like a lot until you realize that, if you dumped it all into barrels and stacked it end to end, you could fit the entirety into a single football-field-sized hole about seven yards deep.[6]

Now let's think about what a single, moderately deep football field looks like compared to the sheer size of the United States. The total surface area of the country is 3,795,967 square miles. How many football fields could you fit into that space? Only about 1,836,344,400 of them. I don't know about you, but I feel like we could spare one football field out of the 1.8 billion for some nuclear waste.

Obviously, I'm simplifying a bit. You're going to need a larger amount of land around the football-field-sized storage facility, but you get the main idea here.

By the way, as we move into the future and all the technological advances it promises, the amount of stored waste will only decrease. Even today, the technology allows for a full 96% of nuclear waste to be recycled into new fuel. The total amount of waste I mentioned above, if recycled into new fuel, could run all of the nuclear reactors in the US for 30 years with no new uranium input.[7]

But what about transporting the waste? Doesn't the act of trucking the stuff from Point A to Point B expose people to unnecessary risk? Well... *no.* "A staggering amount of evidence directly refutes this myth...In the United States, since 1971, more than 20,000 shipments of spent fuel and nuclear waste have been transported more than 18 million miles without incident. Transportation of radioactive materials is just not a problem."[8]

In the end, no matter how you slice it politically, "Nuclear wastes are certainly a significant part of the nuclear power picture and need to be managed and disposed properly... [However] In more than 5 decades of civil nuclear power experience, nuclear wastes have not caused any serious health or environmental problems nor posed any real risks to people."[9]

"Fine then," Team Nuclear's opponents might say. "We can accept that Team Nuclear is a zero-emissions technology that has no real and terrifying impact on air or land pollution. But there is still the real and terrifying danger of nuclear power leading to more nuclear weapons and acts of terrorism."

To that, I say, "Oh, opponents of Team Nuclear, you still have so much to learn."

3. The proliferation of nuclear power doesn't place you at any greater risk of death by explosion.

Some people get nervous about the cooling towers they see on the horizon because they can imagine the whole structure completely collapsing, creating cinema-grade mushroom clouds. I've already addressed the extreme unlikelihood of another Chernobyl or Fukushima event occurring with modern versions of nuclear plants (particularly SMRs that are buried underground), but let's discuss for a minute the preposterous idea that a nuclear plant could explode.

First, a nuclear plant and a nuclear weapon are two totally different things. We've already gone in depth about the differences in the uranium each technology uses, so let's just let the Nuclear Energy Institute sum this one up: "It is physically impossible for a US commercial reactor to explode like a nuclear weapon. The concentration of uranium-235 within the reactor fuel is far too low to be explosive... During power operations, when the temperature within the reactor reaches a predetermined level, the fission process is naturally suppressed so the power level cannot spike under any circumstances. No one could intentionally or unintentionally alter a commercial nuclear reactor, its controls or its fuel to make it explode like a nuclear bomb."[10]

Just in case the above wasn't clear enough: it is not physically possible for a nuclear plant to explode. If this silly myth had you worried about living near a nuclear plant, well, you can rest easy from now on.

Wait, though! *Terrorists!*

Yes, the horror of the World Trade Center collapse on September 11, 2001 has to leave us wondering whether it's possible for someone to hijack a plane, crash it into a nuclear plant, and cause it to explode in such a way as to level entire cities and leave huge swaths of land uninhabitable for centuries.

Attacking a nuclear plant would be a colossal waste of time and resources for anyone wanting to do harm. We already know that, even if suicide terrorists somehow got inside a nuclear plant and took over, they couldn't make it explode like a bomb because the uranium isn't enriched enough to be explosive. Also, no matter what they might use to attack the reactor (passenger jets included), good luck breaching the multiple thick steel and concrete barriers that enclose all US reactors.

How can I be so sure of myself here? Well, for one thing, every test ever run on the subject shows it to be impossible by a vast margin of safety.

Let's just look at one recent study by the Electric Power Research Institute. This particular study concluded that flying a commercial airliner full of fuel directly into a nuclear plant wouldn't exactly be like flying into a building of steel and glass. Rather, it would be like flying into a fortress of solid rock. In fact, even if you ramp up the explosive potential of the jetliner to a much higher level than we saw on September 11, 2001, there's still no penetrating the containment structure.[11]

Okay, but what if someone managed to waltz into a nuclear plant and steal the uranium? Couldn't they do bad things with it? Well, no—and we're back to the issue of how the uranium used in a nuclear plant isn't useful in a nuclear weapon unless it's further enriched (which is a seriously expensive and difficult process). Think about it this way: if you were a bad guy, would you try to orchestrate a daring break-in to a heavily fortified nuclear plant, steal the core of a reactor that keeps all the lights on in the city, make your way out of the country (or at least back to your secret hideout) with the nuclear material in hand, pay for and set up an elaborate and entirely hidden uranium enrichment facility, enrich your stolen uranium, and then harvest that radioactive material for a bomb? Seems like an unnecessarily elaborate and risky plan.

Plus, even if it were possible to break into a nuclear plant in the first place, the security a thief would have to circumvent would be overwhelming. And don't forget that if someone managed to steal the uranium from a nuclear plant, it wouldn't just be the guards who would be alerted by the power outage; it would be every single person in the surrounding area whose lights just went out. The notion that somebody would even *want* to try to steal the uranium from a nuclear plant is, frankly, absurd.

Finally, let's address the elephant in the room. Even if a rogue group of terrorists or a comic-book supervillain can't exactly use our own nuclear plants against us, there's still the fear of nuclear power in the hands of countries that sponsor terrorism.

The United States and Iran have been rattling sabers for years over the accusation that Iran is using its uranium-enriching capabilities for something more than just to generate nuclear power. Some suspect that Iran is using its "peaceful" nuclear power aspirations as a mere cover for the creation of nuclear weapons. So isn't Iran kind of a cautionary tale about what happens if we allow countries that sponsor terrorism to build nuclear plants?

There's a pretty gigantic misconception at play here. It isn't the aspiration to have a nuclear plant that makes Iran seem so dangerous. It's Iran's *uranium enrichment facility* that worries policymakers in the United States. If you have a nuclear plant, then yes, you have uranium in hand. But as we've covered several times already now, that nuclear plant uranium is useless if you're trying to build a nuclear bomb. There's just not enough U-235 in the fuel mix.

On the other hand, if (like Iran) you have access to a uranium enrichment facility, then you can enrich your uranium according to whatever your whims may be, peaceful or otherwise. The same technology Iran uses to enrich uranium for its nuclear power plants can be used to create the 90% U-235 necessary to make a nuclear bomb.

This brings up an interesting point about how peaceful nuclear power could work worldwide. It's not *nuclear plants* we need to regulate countries from building; it's uranium enrichment facilities. Obviously it would be unwise to allow any hostile country to have an enrichment facility, but that doesn't mean we can't allow any country in the world that wants a nuclear plant to purchase the 10% U-235 uranium it needs from globally approved and monitored enrichment centers. You want to build a nuclear plant? Fine. But one of the handful of pre-approved host countries will do all the 10% U-235 uranium enriching for you. This way, no one ever has to worry about you getting any big ideas about building a nuclear weapon by enriching your uranium further.

Thanks to the leadership of the International Atomic Energy Agency, we're already making progress in this direction. There are currently ten facilities in the world that specialize in enrichment of uranium to 10% U-235 for export. Those facilities reside in France,

Germany, Japan, the United States (where four of them exist), Russia, China, and Pakistan.[12]

Remember, it all boils down to this: while a nuclear reactor and a nuclear weapon both use uranium, the uranium for one does not equate to the uranium for the other. With enough oversight and regulation, the benefits of nuclear power can be enjoyed worldwide with peaceful aspirations assured.

Now that we've cleared up the myths about various evildoers trying to blow up your house, we can move on to another common misconception: that every nuclear plant in the world is just one harebrained mistake away from melting down or blowing up entirely by accident.

4. Don't forget about passive safety.

As we learned in chapter 4, the question of safety has always been one of the biggest barriers for Team Nuclear in terms of public sentiment. Many people simply can't in good conscience embrace the idea that they are perfectly safe as long as there is a person manning the controls of a nearby nuclear plant. Visions of some dolt screwing up the shutdown process stand clear in many opponents' minds.

I am the first to admit that human error is a difficult obstacle to overcome. We've all seen "foolproof" technologies that have underestimated man's potential for foolishness. The idea is that, even if we build a computer or a system smarter than a person, it's still a person who built that computer or system, so the possibility of mistakes remains.

So if we can't overcome that potential to screw up, then why don't we just remove the human from the process entirely? "Passive nuclear safety is a safety feature of a nuclear reactor that does not require operator actions or electronic feedback in order to shut down safely in the event of a particular type of emergency (usually overheating resulting from a loss of coolant or loss of coolant flow). Such reactors tend to rely more on the engineering components such that their predicted behavior according to known laws of physics would slow, rather than accelerate, the nuclear reaction in such circumstances."[13]

Don't trust a nuclear technician to do the job? Fine. Don't trust a computer to do the job? Fine. Then how about we let the physics of the reactor shut it down automatically in the event that something goes wrong? There's one thing we know for certain about physics: it behaves according to unbreakable laws. You can screw up a shutdown operation. You can screw up a computer program. But you can't mess with physics. Passive safety eliminates future safety concerns.

5. Nuclear power saves lives—*millions* of them.

Up to this point, we've been addressing an awful lot of negative myths. So let's turn to some positive news no one seems to be talking about: When compared to the deaths that result from the mining and use of fossil fuels—and in particular from coal mining—nuclear power has saved millions of lives.[14]

Let's break that down to real numbers. Worldwide, for every one person that has died from nuclear power plant accidents, 4,000 have died from accidents related to coal power. This means that coal power is 4,000 times deadlier than nuclear power, and yet we let coal plants run on and on without protest over matters of safety.

That doesn't even take into account the number of lives we might have saved if the world ran solely on nuclear power instead of relying so heavily on coal. According to an April 2013 report by NASA scientists, if all of the coal plants in operation over the past 40-plus years had been nuclear plants instead, it would have prevented as many as 7.5 million deaths from respiratory illness, hereditary degradation, heart problems, and cancer attributed to fossil fuel pollution.[15]

If nuclear power is starting to sound like a panacea, my guess is that any doubters among us will turn next to the claim that there's not enough uranium to keep the Team Nuclear operation running for long anyway. Wrong again, doubters!

6. There is enough nuclear fuel on the planet to last forever (or at least as close to "forever" as we can get)

Greenpeace suggests that we're dealing with "relatively limited reserves of uranium worldwide." What does "relatively limited" mean? Apparently it means that raising the prevalence of nuclear plants to where they're producing the majority of electricity worldwide would reduce our potential uranium supply to a measly 12 years.[16] I'm sorry to be so blunt, but if you look at the real numbers, that claim is simply preposterous.

Even if we ignore the potential for improving nuclear fuel consumption technology, "At current consumption levels, known uranium reserves are predicted to last for 85 years."[17] Obviously that number is much, much higher than the 12-year figure Greenpeace likes to quote. It's important to note that we're talking only about *known* uranium reserves here, too. Even if the planet collectively refuses to spend one more dime on uranium exploration, we've got enough uranium to finish out the century. And if we decide it might be worth the effort to go looking for more? "Geological estimates from the International Atomic Energy Agency and the Organisation for Economic Cooperation and Development show that at least six times more uranium is extractable—enough for 500 years' supply at current demand."[18]

Now here's where the discussion gets downright biblical. We've covered the fact that nuclear fuel can't be used to make a bomb without first committing to the difficult and expensive enrichment process. The flip side of this is that it's cheap and relatively simple to blend military-grade uranium with naturally occurring uranium into a mix that works as fuel for a nuclear plant. What does all this mean? It means you can't use nuclear plant uranium to create a nuclear bomb, but you *can* use nuclear bomb uranium to help fuel a nuclear plant. Even as we disable the world's nuclear warheads, we can use that extracted uranium to create more zero-emissions electricity in our nuclear power plants. Bombs gone; greenhouse gases reduced.

Does this sound too good to be true? Well it isn't. In fact, it's already happening, and has been happening since way back in 1987.

That's the year the United States and Russia (which was still the Soviet Union back then) struck a series of agreements to disarm their nuclear weapons to use the uranium for peaceful nuclear power purposes. Known as "Megatons for Megawatts," those landmark agreements are a bit like a modern-day version of the biblical "swords into ploughshares."[19] The agreement has worked quite well since the late '80s, too. By 2009, a full 50% of the fuel in American reactors came from dismantled nuclear bombs, and 45 of this 50% came from *Russian* warheads. This total accounts for about a tenth of all electricity generated in the United States.

In summary, we've got as many as 500 years' worth of uranium that we can extract from the Earth, and we've got all those nuclear warheads to disarm and use for fuel as well. Don't forget thorium, either. Thorium can be found in far greater abundance even than plentiful uranium. Plus, it works more efficiently than uranium as a nuclear fuel, is safer in operation, reduces the risk of nuclear weapons proliferation, and leads to less nuclear waste. So as we progress toward greater acceptance of thorium reactor technology, the whole conversation about uranium availability becomes less and less relevant.

When we talk about the hundreds of years' worth of uranium and the thousands of years' worth of thorium we can find in the ground, we still haven't discussed the thousands and even tens of thousands of years of uranium we could harvest from the world's oceans. Considering the vastness of the oceans and the significant quantities of uranium contained therein, it doesn't seem a stretch to suggest that we've got enough uranium on this planet to last us nearly forever.

7. Thanks to advances in technology, the up-front cost to build a nuclear plant is becoming more manageable all the time.

For large nuclear power plants (the ones with the big cooling towers), the vast majority of cost is up front. Once the government or a private entity has made the investment to build the plant, the costs thereafter are quite low. Sure, there are ongoing expenses, but those expenses are far less than for a coal or natural gas plant.

There was a time when the up-front costs for a nuclear plant represented a major hurdle—one that almost always required government subsidy to overcome. SMRs will eliminate that hurdle altogether. This is because SMR design and production will eventually be cookie cutter, making production more efficient and lower in cost. Indeed, "SMRs can reduce a nuclear plant owner's capital investment due to the lower plant capital cost. Modular components and factory fabrication can reduce construction costs and duration."[20] I have already asked you to picture a manufacturing plant rolling out SMRs on an assembly line. Well, that reality is imminent.

These factors open up a whole new world of possibility for Team Nuclear. If you make a smaller, less expensive version of a nuclear plant, then the barrier to investment for private entities is eliminated.

Even if SMRs don't wind up making the impact I anticipate, we're still looking at a world where the up-front costs don't appear to be a significant enough barrier to entry. How do I know this? Because there are just so many of these supposedly "too expensive" nuclear reactors in operation, under construction, or in development at the time of this writing. How many exactly? There are 438 large nuclear reactors in operation, with 69 more under construction, 184 planned, and 312 proposed for future construction sometime between now and 2030. These numbers represent 22 nations with large nuclear plants currently in operation and 17 more planning to join the parade.[21]

Also, if the financial hurdles for nuclear power are so high, then why is it true that so many utility companies with a history of using nuclear power are actively seeking to *buy* existing nuclear plants? Why are they spending so much money upgrading these plants they own or are purchasing? Why are they extending their operating licenses?[22] You don't do any of these things if you believe nuclear technology has no future.

As for the expensiveness of nuclear power from a consumer perspective, the cost of a large nuclear power plant is wrapped up almost entirely in construction expenses, interest on capital loans, and salaries for managers and plant operators.[23] Even if we can assume that Team Nuclear's construction costs will remain higher than those of the other teams in the conference (and we can't, since assembly-line SMRs will change the game completely), nuclear power is only marginally more expensive than natural gas at historically normal prices and cheaper than current wind and solar power.[24] With the predicted rises in fuel cost and carbon footprint penalties over the coming decades, it's only a matter of time before electricity from coal and natural gas becomes more expensive than electricity from nuclear power as well.[25]

8. Team Nuclear has a size for every occasion.

Every team in the Electricity Conference suffers from the same problem: they need space (a large amount of it, in most cases) to operate. Because of the often dangerous nature of electricity production, that space usually has to occupy remote areas, meaning that long transmission lines must be constructed to deliver the electricity where it is needed. This can be a costly operation both in terms of money and electricity loss.

This is exactly why Team Nuclear's tremendous ability to come in all shapes and sizes is such an advantage. From a traditional large reactor with tall concrete towers to an SMR the size of a hot tub, Team Nuclear has the size to get the job done. If you want to deliver additional power to a city with little land to spare, there's an SMR to meet your needs. In addition, it's buried in the ground, and no one will ever know it's there. Such an SMR could serve from 20,000 to as many as 300,000 people. If your energy needs expand, you can always add an additional SMR as well, since the whole system is modular. And if you have to get power to an entire region, there's still the large plant to meet the electricity needs of up to three million people.

9. The potential for technological advancement is virtually limitless.

For the past few decades or so, if you wanted to know about the potential of a new technology, one excellent resource to consult has been Bill Gates. Gates has either been at the helm for some of the world's most groundbreaking technology advancements, has influenced them indirectly, or has predicted them long before anyone else saw them coming. He is arguably one of the top visionaries of our time. And he loves what he sees in nuclear power.

Gates called nuclear technology *disruptive*, meaning that technological advancements in nuclear power could shake up and revolutionize the way we produce and deliver electricity to the world. The reason? "Gates said that one of the best aspects of nuclear power at the moment is its lack of innovation thus far, which leaves it ripe for disruption in the coming years."[26] What he means by "lack of innovation" is that projections suggest nuclear power has only reached 20% of its capacity for efficiency and effectiveness in delivering huge amounts of reliable electricity, 24 hours a day. There is no other team in the Electricity Conference that has so much room to get better and better.

When compared to all other methods for producing electricity, nuclear power has enormously greater potential for disrupting the status quo with technological advancement. As I mentioned earlier, in addition to SMRs, one of the most exciting projected advancements in nuclear technology is the adoption of thorium as a nuclear fuel—and Bill Gates agrees. "Some believe thorium is key to developing a new generation of cleaner, safer nuclear power... considering its overall potential, thorium-based power 'can mean a 1,000+ year solution or a quality low-carbon bridge to truly sustainable energy sources solving a huge portion of mankind's negative environmental impact.'"[27]

This isn't exactly a new concept either. In fact, there was a reactor running on thorium in the United States as early as 1965.[28] The government shut down research on this reactor technology in 1973, however, because new uranium reactors seemed like the more efficient technology to pursue at the time. If you dig a little deeper into the history of the concept, you will find that thorium reactor technology was shut down in part because thorium isn't useful in bomb making. The government, in other words, influenced the direction of nuclear plant technology in part to facilitate nuclear bomb development in connection with the nuclear arms race.

These days, thanks in large part to Terra Power, a company established and funded by the Bill & Melinda Gates Foundation, there's plenty of money behind the technology. Terra Power is currently in the process of creating a new kind of nuclear reactor called a Traveling Wave Reactor (TWR). The technology is scheduled to come online in the mid-2020s, meaning that this could be an additional advantage for Team Nuclear on par with SMRs.[29]

It all began back in 2006, when Gates assembled a group of top nuclear scientists with the goal to create efficient and affordable clean energy. "This group concluded that the best option for addressing the world's growing energy challenges was to expand the utilization of nuclear energy, in a more suitable form, on a global basis."[30] The reactor concept they developed utilizes the fuel in "waves," which is a fancy way of saying that it uses nearly all of the fuel while producing exceedingly small amounts of waste. It is so efficient in its fuel use, in fact, that a TWR uses only one tenth as much uranium as any other modern nuclear reactor. If this kind of reactor becomes as widespread as Gates believes it will, then that factor alone would reduce the amount of uranium a country would need to mine or import by ten times.

But that's not all! Not only does a TWR consume almost all of its fuel while producing almost no waste, it can also operate effectively while using existing nuclear waste as fuel. So any stored waste produced by past or current nuclear reactors could be recycled as usable fuel in a TWR. Amazing! All the nuclear waste in the United States—and indeed in the world—could be reduced to nearly zero. And while we're removing all that waste from the planet, that same waste is providing enough electricity to power every single US household for the next 700 years. *700 years!*[31]

In addition to virtually eliminating nuclear waste, TWRs feature a number of key improvements and advantages that will further Team Nuclear's chances of winning the conference in the coming decades. First, these reactors use naturally occurring uranium (U-238) as their fuel. This means there is no enrichment necessary, which of course means that we would no longer need enrichment facilities, which in turn means that we could virtually eliminate the fear that expanding nuclear power would also allow certain countries to gain nuclear weapons. As a bonus, since 15% of the operating cost for a nuclear power plant is associated with enriching its fuel, the fact that a TWR employs naturally occurring uranium would reduce that operating cost by 15%. Some if not all of this new efficiency could be passed on to the consumer.[32]

Next, TWRs improve safety measures across the board. They will all have passive safety systems, where the laws of physics prevent any out-of-control heat situations—no offsite electricity or human intervention required. Also, unlike other modern nuclear reactors, they do not need to operate under high-pressure conditions, which means it isn't possible for an accident to occur as the result of a loss of air pressure.

The logistics of running a TWR also present major advantages. For instance, this kind of reactor cools its reactions with air circulation, which eliminates the need for huge cooling towers. Once fueled, the core of a TWR is so efficient and self-sufficient that it can remain closed for up to 40 years. Rather than water, a TWR uses sodium to transfer heat from the reactor to the generator. This is a key point to note because sodium can be heated safely to a higher temperature than water, which adds to the safety factor while also generating electricity at greater efficiency.[33]

The fact is that, out of any team in the conference, Team Nuclear stands the greatest chance of technological development—and it's really not even a close race. This is partly because of the factors outlined above, and partly because there is so much more about nuclear power yet to be discovered. Meanwhile, wind is wind. The sun is the sun. Water is water. Coal is coal. Natural gas is natural gas. Sure, you might see a few improvements in harvesting and storing electricity from some of these technologies (wind and solar in particular), but with none of them will you see the same level of potential improvement enjoyed by Team Nuclear.

10. Nuclear power already has far more support than you may realize.
After reading all these positives for Team Nuclear, you might be wondering why so many people are against building new nuclear

plants. The answer here is simple: most people are in fact *in favor* of building new nuclear plants. So what gives?

It all starts with one of the most common political tactics known to man: if you don't favor something, just spend as much money as you can on a campaign that turns the lie into the publicly accepted fact. In this case, there are twin lies at play. The first is that most Americans hold unfavorable opinions about the technology. The second is that there is a strict divide between the two major political parties about whether nuclear energy is something we should pursue.

On the contrary, according to recent surveys, 70% of Americans responded that they support nuclear power. Even more people—84% to be exact—suggested that they envision nuclear power making a significant contribution to electricity in the future. Another 70% of respondents said they would support the idea of the nearest nuclear plant deciding to build additional reactors.[34]

I'm no mathematician, but it seems to me that with numbers like 70%, 84%, and 70%, Americans are in fact overwhelmingly in favor of nuclear power. Could it be that the vocal minority and the media are merely winning the war of words here? Could it be that Team Nuclear is already even stronger than many people realize?

When thinking about Team Nuclear's ability to provide cheap electricity to a large consumer base while producing *no* greenhouse gases, it is difficult to exaggerate just how much this technology could positively impact the world. It is, as I have stated already, the same kind of game-changing advancement we saw with the introduction of the internal combustion engine, the computer, and the Internet. Such advancements changed billions of lives by making the world smaller, more accessible, and better connected, thus increasing the standard of living. They changed the face of business, ultimately leading to a demand for electricity with which mankind has demonstrated some difficulty in keeping up (at least to date).

From an electricity perspective, nuclear power, and SMRs in particular, can deliver the world's 1.5 billion people currently living without electricity out of the dark and into the light.[35] Team Nuclear can do this even as it replaces coal and natural gas plants that contribute so much greenhouse gas and particulate matter into the atmosphere, thus combating global warming and improving the overall environmental picture. Zero emissions and economic stimulation: it is for these reasons that Team Nuclear is the clear and obvious winner of the Electricity Conference.

The question now is: who will win the Fuel Conference and square off against Team Nuclear in the Clean Energy Bowl?

The "Three Cs" of Ethanol: Cars, Crude Oil, and Corn

With this chapter, we'll switch focus and concentrate on why I believe Team Ethanol will be the winner of the Fuel Conference. To meet this end, I intend to do three things.

First, I will demonstrate that, despite what the hype might lead you to believe, the internal combustion engine (ICE) isn't going away. In fact, its numbers will increase dramatically in the coming decades.

Second, I will demonstrate that the world will reach the point where oil production peaks and begins to decline. Every year after that peak, we will see a choppy downward trend in global oil production, which will lead to a rise in the cost for a gallon of gasoline.*

Finally, I will offer a scenario in which corn—a key ingredient for producing ethanol—will not see the same rise in cost of production. In fact, my scenario provides a model of corn production in which corn will remain at or near historical price levels.

As a quick aside, I should note that corn isn't the only crop that can be used to create ethanol. Another particularly effective crop is sugarcane. In tropical countries like Brazil, sugarcane is the chief crop used to make ethanol. In the United States, there are regions where planting sugarcane could help the overall ethanol production picture. But for the purposes of this chapter, I'm going to focus mostly on corn, which is a crop better suited to the world's more temperate regions (which is where the majority of the available agricultural land in the United States resides).

---

* To describe the above notion, I'm going to be using the term *peak oil* throughout this chapter. Peak oil is that point at which maximum oil production is reached and then gradually declines. The decline curve forecast by leading oil-monitoring agencies is startlingly steep, so that's not a positive omen for Team Gasoline.

These three Cs—cars, crude, and corn—add up to a clear picture of ethanol as surely the wave of the future in the Fuel Conference.

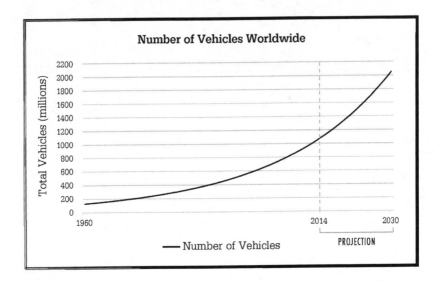

Underlying all three of those points is the trend you see in the chart above. That's the actual number of cars driven worldwide since 1960, projected out to 2030.[1] The graph accounts for all vehicles, regardless of size or engine type, and the projections are based on global GDP and population growth trends. We see this steep upward trajectory because as emerging economic powers like Brazil, China, India, Southeast Asia, South America, and other countries continue to grow their populations and economies, so too will their demand for vehicles grow.

As you can see from the chart, the present-day number of cars driven worldwide is about one billion. Recent research projects that the number of cars will increase to two billion by 2030.

The Internal Combustion Engine Will Dominate

The thought that the number of cars will reach a stunning two billion by 2030 doesn't exactly prove my statement that the ICE will continue to dominate, though, does it? A few other types of engine have indeed emerged in recent years to compete with the ICE, and it's competition we can't simply ignore. However, as I will demonstrate, no matter how many different engines get introduced to the market, the ICE will continue to be the dominant engine worldwide, and by a wide margin.

There are a number of reasons for this. Chief among them is that, even though technological innovation tends to change the game for many products and even industries, the ICE will remain ahead of the engine pack thanks to modern computer design, advanced machine tooling, an increasingly talented team of engineers, new materials, and a hundred-year head start on technological innovation. These are considerable advantages.

The government has set its standard for engine efficiency at 54.5 mpg by 2025.[2] The auto industry has said they can meet that standard. In fact, world automakers are already selling 15 small ICE cars that are knocking on the door of 54.5 mpg if they haven't surpassed that standard already. The leading companies producing these cars are Fiat, Ford, Honda, Mazda, Renault, Toyota, Volkswagen, and Volvo. Also, British car maker Trident, in an example of improved ICE efficiency, built a car competitive in power and design to luxury sports cars like Ferrari, Lamborghini, and Maserati while still getting 50 mpg. The Trident Iceni Grand Tourer is certainly as efficient as it is gorgeous, but it's also extremely expensive, starting at a cool $119,000.[3]

Continuous improvement in ICE efficiency for cars of all sizes, and with prices often lower than alternative-engine cars, could make every other kind of engine (hybrids, plug-in hybrids, electric, and so on) less competitive and perhaps even noncompetitive. Note the graph below:

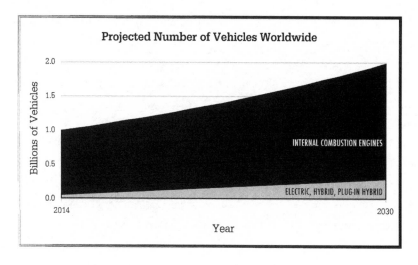

With world automotive sales expected to double between 2010 and 2030, my research projects that the sales of alternative engines like electric, hybrid, and plug-in hybrid will still have a low rate of increase during that same timeframe. "How can this be?" you might ask. "You see it everywhere on TV and the Internet: everyone's buying hybrid and electric cars."

Don't believe the hype. Alternative engines haven't experienced raging sales of late. "The evidence is growing stronger: Average American consumers aren't impressed enough with electric vehicles and plug-in hybrids to pay the kind of prices automakers are charging."[4] And if the numbers can be believed, that's not about to change much.

Way back in 2000, when Toyota first introduced the Prius, we did see a push toward more hybrid and electric vehicles. The interest in such vehicles rose considerably until 2008, when the economic recession led to the industry's first decline. The trouble with the statement "everyone's buying hybrid and electric cars" is that, since 2008, even as companies like Toyota have introduced new technologies and even as global auto sales have started to recover, hybrid cars have represented merely an approximate four percent of new car production. This despite the fact that, during long stretches of time during that period, gasoline prices reached nearly five dollars per gallon in some parts of the United States. The truth is that, in the latter half of the past decade, hybrid vehicles suffered through remarkably low and relatively unchanging demand. As of 2015, hybrid and electric cars still aren't doing as well as predicted because gasoline prices have fallen, giving an advantage to ICEs.

Sales for electric cars are particularly dismal. Today, US roads are packed with 254 million cars. 15.4 million of those cars were sold in 2013. In that same year, the electric car market saw the sale of only 23,094 Chevrolet Volts and 22,610 Nissan Leafs. That's one electric car for every 161 ICEs sold in the United States. So much for media hype.

The percentage of hybrid and electric vehicles on the road hasn't increased much in terms of percentage of all new car sales from 2013 to 2015 and isn't likely to grow much over the next 15 years, either. There are many reasons for this, including the fact that the increase in shale oil production over the coming years will keep the gas price lower than it has been in the immediate past. In fact, if this trend continues, the narrative for electric cars may return to that "it's too soon" message, just like in 2001, when the General Motors electric car died because it just wasn't profitable to make it.

But the most important reason that hybrid and electric cars won't grow much in the coming years is that, over this same period, newly developed ICE technology will allow the ICE to meet or surpass the fuel efficiency of some alternative-engine cars—and it'll do it all at a lower cost to boot.

Given the data I've analyzed, my theory regarding little growth in demand for hybrid and electric cars is simple: all we need do is look at Europe to see how they have solved the problem of high gas prices and the environmental crisis. First, at the time of this writing, the average price per gallon of gasoline for countries in Europe is $7.51, with a high of $10.12 in Norway and a low of $5.71 in Romania (these high prices are largely a result of the high tax rates for gasoline in these countries). Because the gas prices are so high, ICE cars in Europe have gotten smaller and lighter, which has led to dramatic improvements in mpg efficiency. They are already at an average of 44 mpg, not far from the average of 54.5 mpg that the United States set as standard for 2025.[5]

Second, Europe has concentrated on building small, low-emission cars that meet environmental demands. Since their small ICE cars are achieving about the same mpg as a Prius hybrid, and the Prius costs much more, there is virtually no demand for hybrid cars in Europe. "While in 2001 only two hybrid vehicle models were offered in [the European Union], and only about 2,000 were sold, more than 30 hybrid models are now on offer and more than 130,000 are sold."[6] That might sound like a positive trend, but keep in mind that, in 2013, 13 million cars were sold in the EU. So if 13 million were sold, and only 130,000 of those were hybrids, that means only 1 out of every 100 cars sold had a hybrid engine. Put another way, even with gasoline averaging $7.51 per gallon, hybrid cars represented just 1% of all new cars sold in the European Union in 2013.

In Japan, the purchase of hybrids rapidly increased back in the days when the government was heavily subsidizing them. When those subsidies ended, the sale of hybrids moderated and recently began a downward trend. The US government has some subsidies for electrics and hybrids, but those subsidies are beginning to end as well. To see what will happen when subsidies disappear, look no further than the Toyota Prius. In 2010, the US government ended subsidies for purchase of the Prius, and sales for the car have been in decline ever since.[7]

As the United States builds smaller and lighter cars to meet the 54.5 mpg standard, it's easy to figure out what will happen to sales of hybrid and electric cars: a few environmentalists (and others who don't care about the higher price) will continue to buy them, but compared to the number of ICE cars sold over the coming years, hybrid and electric car sales will face modest growth at best. The primary reason for such comparatively small sales of hybrids and electrics appears to have little to do with the green initiative and more to do with economics. To become a hybrid or electric car owner, it seems you need at least one of the following three traits:

1. You have to be more "earth conscious" than the average consumer.
2. You have to be willing to pay substantially more for your hybrid or electric car than for the same model automobile with a standard ICE.
3. You have to have some private company or government subsidies.

The cost extends beyond the premium for the engine. Insurance for hybrids and electrics is more expensive,[8] and the price for repairing them is higher because the parts are more expensive and the repairs require highly trained mechanics.[9]

According to some studies, the premium just for the engine of an average hybrid car can be as much as $8,000.[10] For current models of electric cars, that number is even higher (assuming a comparable-size car). At the time of this writing, the average price for a new ICE Chevrolet Cruze is about $17,000. That price affords the buyer an EPA-rated combined city/highway mileage of 30 mpg. The average price for a new Chevrolet Volt, which is essentially the electric version of the Cruze, is about $41,000. That $24,000 difference can take you 205,000 miles at $3.50 per gallon in the Cruze. Meanwhile, the average price for a hybrid Leaf is $35,000. The $18,000 difference can take you 111,000 miles in the Cruze.

Hybrid Cars and Electric Cars Will Fail

Before we get into depth on the price pressures that will cause hybrid and electric car sales to suffer in the coming years, let me just acknowledge the difficulties in writing about such a subject in this particular media. I'm going to be comparing the costs of current-model hybrid and electric cars to current-model ICE cars, but "current models" change every year. For this reason, we have to keep in mind that the price differences between alternative engines and ICEs may change from year to year, but the concept I'm presenting here remains the same. No matter what the exact numbers wind up being in the years to come, hybrids and electrics will continue to be more expensive than comparable high-mpg ICE cars like the ones discussed above. This will be especially true in times when hybrid and electric subsidies disappear.

Now, with that disclaimer behind us, we can move on to the good stuff.

Why is the sticker price for hybrid and electric cars so much higher? In a word, batteries. The idea that you could drive a car on less or no gas, using an engine propelled partially or even entirely by a rechargeable battery, all without experiencing any drop-off in performance or mileage, is quite attractive. The barrier to achieving this appears to be twofold, however. First, the batteries currently running hybrids and electrics are too costly for them to compete with the ICE. Second, current-model technology isn't effective enough to render the cars as reliable and capable as Americans have come to expect. In the coming years, it is probable that the technology will improve. It is also probable that the expense issue will get worse, especially with the greater efficiency we can expect to see in the ICE over that same time period.

Even if we assume there is no cost to charge your Leaf or Volt every night (there is a cost, but let's ignore it), you would have to drive the Leaf for 12 years before you saved enough on gas to make up for that $18,000 price premium over the Chevy Cruze, and for 17 years to make up for the Volt's $24,000 premium.[**]

It's easy enough to reveal the current differences in sticker price and the future trends regarding battery production and raw materials and call this a win for the ICE. The truly savvy objector, however, would point out that

---

[**] As I mentioned, these premiums are due almost entirely to the cost of the battery needed to propel an electric car. Until and unless the production methods and necessary materials come down in price, we will continue to see staggeringly high costs for the batteries. And until and unless those batteries become substantially better and cheaper, we'll be paying a great deal more for alternative engines that perform at a far lower level than the ICE.

up-front cost isn't everything. These hybrid and electric cars are supposed to save a great deal of money in the long run. You have to spend an extra $8,000 to $24,000 up front, but given that you will be purchasing far less (or in the case of electric cars, absolutely no) gasoline during the lifetime of that vehicle, you will easily recoup the extra cost in the long run. Right?

Let's start with hybrids—and if you're a fan of these engines, I have to warn you that you're in for a rude awakening. While it's true that hybrids are typically among the most fuel efficient of all cars available today (the Toyota Prius boasts 48 mpg), their advantage is actually far slimmer than most people might realize.

Take the Honda Civic, for example. The Civic is one of the most popular cars in the United States. The reason for this appears to be twofold. The Honda Civic has a great sticker price at $16,000 (depending on options) and excellent gas mileage for an ICE (36 mpg estimated). Compare that to the Toyota Prius, which has a sticker price of $24,000 and an estimated 48 mpg.

For your 12-mpg increase, you're paying an additional $8,000 up front. Let's assume you buy the Toyota Prius. At purchase, you are officially $8,000 in the red versus what you would have spent on the Civic. Let's say you then drive the same mileage as the average American (12,000 miles per year at $3.50 per gallon of gas). This means that driving a Civic for a full year will cost you $1,166 in gas money. Driving that same distance in your new Prius will cost you only $875. That's a $291 savings in one year. Not too shabby, certainly, but you haven't even made a dent in your $8,000 up-front premium.

In fact, a dent doesn't start to show until you've driven your new hybrid for five whole years. But a dent is still just a dent. At five years, you're still $6,545 behind. At ten years, you're still $5,090 behind. Not until your 27th year of owning your hybrid will you have fully recouped the extra $8,000 you paid up front—and by then (if it's not dead already), you'll be rolling the dilapidated old thing into the junkyard.

If we compare the Honda Civic to the Honda Civic Hybrid, we get essentially the same result. With the boost from 36 mpg to a mere 44 mpg, you won't recoup that added premium of $8,000 in the purchase price until you've driven it for 38 years.

So sure, hybrid cars might save you money in the very, very long run. And they are, on average, 37% "better for the environment" in terms of emissions. But do you really want to drive the same car for 27 or even 38 years?

Remember, while all these expensive hybrids are failing to live up to their promises to save you money, car companies are producing internal combustion engines that get up to 54.5 mpg in smaller and lighter cars. One of the innovations that has allowed them to get to this high number is to shut down four of the engine's eight cylinders when less engine power is required (for example, at a stop light).[11] So as you can see, by the time cars with these engines go out to the public, the mpg advantage of the much more expensive hybrid will likely have been narrowed considerably, and in some cases completely eliminated.

Now on to the electric car.

If you buy an electric vehicle, you'll never pay for gasoline again. But keep in mind that the up-front price premium of the Nissan Leaf over the Honda Civic is around $19,000. Estimates place the electricity cost at an average of five cents per mile. If we assume the same 12,000 miles per year of driving and the same $3.50 gallon of gas average, it will take about 25 years to recoup the up-front price premium you paid for the Leaf. Remember, every extra dollar you send to the electric company each month also cuts into your savings margin.

Repairs for an electric car can be brutal as well. For one thing, if your battery ever breaks down on the interstate—or even if one connection between the battery and the engine is broken—you'll have to call a tow truck to take you to the nearest dealer that can supply you with a new battery. Forget about carrying an extra battery with you to avoid this kind of scenario, too. Current-model batteries for an electric car are extremely bulky, weighing in at over a thousand pounds.[12]

And then there is the matter of actually charging the battery. The problem here is threefold. First, charging the battery on a current-model electric engine takes up to eight hours. That pretty much leaves you with only a few opportunities for regular charging: (1) you can charge it at home overnight (a home charging station costs $2,000), (2) you can be lucky enough to have an employer who will provide you access to a charging station while you're at work, or (3) you can wheel your electric car over to the local library, church, or other public place that offers a charging station. The second problem is that the range on a typical charge is 150 miles. So there is simply no way to take an electric on a long road trip. And what if you forget to charge the battery one night? You could find yourself stuck at home for hours, waiting for the battery to charge enough to get you to work.

Which leads us directly to the third problem. While you might be seeing electric car charging stations popping up here and there in public places, the numbers are nothing compared to the 121,466 gas stations around the United States.[13]

My arguments above don't even get into the prediction that government support for alternative engines will wane, or that there are serious safety concerns to consider when you're driving a car powered by electricity (when a hybrid or electric is involved in an accident, you and your rescuers will find yourselves in danger of being electrocuted).[14]

I also haven't pointed out the performance issues of hybrids in particular. Because their combination of ICE infrastructure and batteries weighs so much, hybrids are often much heavier than their ICE counterparts. This makes for slower and generally sloppier handling. In response to this common problem, many manufacturers have taken to the strategy of reducing the weight of their hybrids' engines in an effort to compensate for the added weight of the battery. The result? A less powerful engine. So if you like cars that drive fast or corner well, a hybrid isn't for you.

For all of these reasons and more, it seems safe to say that the ICE will remain king for the foreseeable future—and the data clearly backs this notion. At present, hybrids and electrics account for a mere 4% of world auto sales.[15] Even if that share increased to 10% by 2030, we're still looking at a drop in the bucket. The owner of that other 90% of world market share? The good old (and yet substantially new and much-higher-mpg) ICE.

And what will the ICE run on? Two things: gasoline and ethanol. So let's look at the prospects of the raw materials necessary for gasoline and ethanol production: crude oil and corn, respectively.

The World Will Reach the Point of Peak Oil

When it comes to future projections of oil availability, only one thing needs to be said: oil production in the world will reach a peak and begin to decline. As I mentioned, that point is called *peak oil*. Given the findings of studies conducted on worldwide oil wells, reserves, and oil fields, it appears that the decline will be at least as rapid as was the increase. Once peak oil is reached, some global oil agencies and experts believe that oil production could drop by as much as 6% per year—and frankly, that's a terrifying thought.[16]

Well hold on to your hats, because it's already kind of happening. For one thing, many of the world's conventional oil wells (which are oil wells that drill directly into pools of oil) already have reached peak and are declining significantly. Recent research shows that conventional world oil production is the same in 2014 as it was in 2005. Put another way, while we might not be able to officially call this a peak quite yet, we're definitely looking at a plateau. And indeed, that plateau has probably only been able to occur because of shale oil production. I contend that, without that added bonus of shale oil, the world would have surpassed the peak already.

Largely because of this shale oil "bonus," by the way, some people are saying that the concept of peak oil is dead. In reply, I say, "No it's not. It's just sleeping." Once the shale oil is gone (which will happen sooner than most people think), peak oil will wake up again.

Below you'll find the concept of peak oil in its simplest charted form.

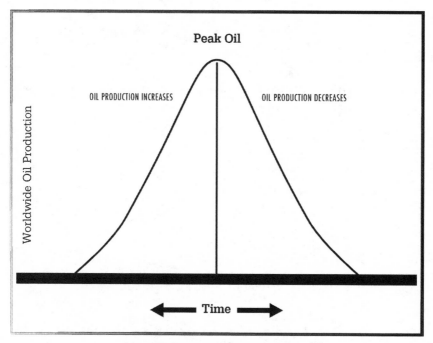

Source: BP Statistical Review of World Energy

Some suggest that the debate about peak oil is a silly one because it's impossible to truly predict how much oil there is to be found on Earth. While it's true that it's difficult to predict the amount, it's certainly not impossible to make some reasonable estimates based on what we know now. Here's what we know now: every decade since 1960, there have been fewer new discoveries of oil. The lone exception to that rule is the current decade, with the period between 2010 and 2020 experiencing an increase reflecting the recoverable shale oil in the world.[17]

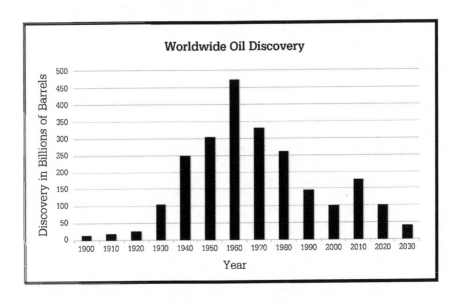

No matter what you believe about the potential for shale oil, it's clear that, in 1964, new conventional oil discoveries reached nearly 500 billion barrels.[18] Recently, that number dropped to just above 20 billion barrels per year.[19] With less and less easily extractable oil being discovered—and with oil wells currently in use containing a finite amount of oil—it seems safe to say that, even with a temporary boost from shale oil, at some point world supply is in for a rapid decline.

Shale Is Not the Savior

While we're on the subject of oil, we've probably beat around the bush long enough: shale drilling and fracking has many people in the oil industry quite excited about what that new shale oil might add to the picture. In recent years, we've seen any number of projections anointing oil from shale as everything from the wave of the future to the savior of the American economy. In short, I think the prognosticators in the oil industry would do well to temper their enthusiasm a bit.

When we talk about oil from shale, what we're really talking about are two things: shale oil and oil shale. Confusing, I know—so confusing, in fact, that many experts have failed to distinguish between the two. That failure has led to grossly inaccurate projections regarding just how much oil we can expect to get out of these massive shale formations beneath the surface of the United States. Some suggest that these US shale formations boast *three times* as much oil as Saudia Arabia has.[20] Others believe there is as much oil in the shale formations in the United States as there is oil in the rest of the world combined.[21]

To hear some people tell it, just as we're on the brink of peak oil worldwide, we've suddenly "discovered" oil heaven right here at home. No more paying money to countries that support terrorism. No more high gas prices. People who own the shale oil land will become enormously rich. We'll get 200 billion barrels of oil from shale oil and another 1.5 *trillion* barrels from oil shale. With our 1.7 trillion barrels of domestic oil, we won't need OPEC anymore. As a result, gasoline and other petroleum derivatives will become plentiful and cheap. It will be the boom to end all booms.

Unfortunately, none of this is true, and it's all based on a fundamental misunderstanding about what shale oil and oil shale *are*.

Let's start with shale oil. Shale oil is a porous rock that contains usable liquid oil extractable through a complicated process called *horizontal drilling* and/or *fracking*. These two drilling approaches make environmentalists cringe due to their tendency to produce greenhouse gases and pollute groundwater and air in and around drilling sites, but that's beside the point. The point I'd like to concentrate on here is that some estimates put the amount of shale oil beneath the United States at 200 billion barrels. That might sound like a lot, but when you start to break down the true numbers, the picture isn't quite so rosy.[22] Unfortunately, those 200-billion-barrel projections fail to take into account the noted depletion rate of the average shale oil well.[23]

Here's what the depletion rate looks like in chart form:[24]

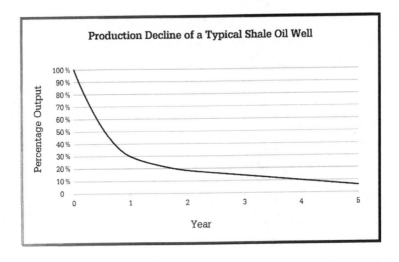

If you're an investor, that's not the kind of line you want to see on a chart. It means that immediate returns might look nice, but in just one year, those returns will plummet. The left side of that chart is what the folks in the shale oil industry have used to come up with their 200 billion barrel projection. But as you can see, the wake-up call will come in less than a year. According to my calculations, as a result of the depletion rate, those 200 billion projected barrels of oil will actually turn out to be something in the neighborhood of only 24 billion barrels.*** That might still seem like a nice amount of oil, but do keep that number in mind, because I'm going to debunk its significance shortly.

First, though, let's turn to oil shale.

It's strange that they call it oil shale, because it actually contains no oil. What it contains instead is a solid organic carbon material called *kerogen*. As I mentioned, some have projected that we'll be able to obtain as many as 1.5 trillion barrels of oil from oil shale. Again, this is a projection seen through rose-colored glasses—one that does not take into account the reality of how difficult and expensive it is to create actual, usable, liquid oil from oil shale.

Liquid is the active word in that previous sentence. The problem with kerogen is that you can't just toss it into your gas tank and hit the road. First

---

*** By the way, you might want to check the endnotes on oil depletion, because there are some graphs that show depletion rates *even more rapid* than I'm depicting above. One of the big surprises that will come as a result of these rapid depletion rates is that the US will be back to importing a large percentage of its oil within ten to fifteen years.

you have to heat it to an extremely high temperature, which converts it to liquid oil. Without that heat, kerogen is useless to oil companies. And as oil megacompany ExxonMobil discovered as long ago as 1985, drilling for kerogen and then heating it to 700 degrees Fahrenheit to produce liquid oil just isn't cost effective enough to make for a profitable product.[25]

ExxonMobil isn't alone, either. Chevron has abandoned its lease on oil shale located in northwest Colorado.[26] Randy Udall, head of the Community Office for Resource Efficiency in Aspen, put it succinctly when he said, "Chevron's research hardly got started and they quickly concluded that they were throwing money down a rabbit hole. It's indicative of the fact that oil and gas companies see much more profitable, and realistic, opportunities elsewhere."[27] Chevron got out before it buried decades of failed research into the project. Royal Dutch Shell PLC spent 31 years experimenting on oil shale extraction in western Colorado, only to pull the plug recently.[28] As all three of these oil giants discovered the hard way, it's just too difficult and expensive to produce any oil from oil shale.

In the end, what have we learned? First, that we were promised 200 billion barrels of oil from shale oil and 1.5 trillion barrels of oil from oil shale, totaling 1.7 trillion barrels of oil. Second, that because the process of converting kerogen to usable oil is so expensive, we're going to get very little if any of that 1.5-trillion-barrel estimate. Third, that due to the depletion rate of shale oil wells, we'll only get 24 billion barrels from shale oil. In other words, instead of 1.7 trillion barrels, we can expect to see about 24 billion barrels of actual, usable, affordable oil. Keep in mind that we can't expect to see all 24 billion barrels at once, either. I project that it will take ten to fifteen years before we get to it all.

But just for fun, let's imagine that it's somehow magically possible to extract all that oil at one time. Presto, we have 24 billion barrels of oil in the US we can use now. Great! What are we going to do with all this awesome new oil? Well, not a lot.

Let's put that number into perspective. The US consumes 7 billion barrels of oil per year. So even if we can get that 24 billion barrels all at the same time, we're still looking at about three to four years' worth of usable oil.

The numbers that include all the oil from oil shale production worldwide aren't any rosier either. The world consumes 30 billion barrels of oil per year, but the projected total amount of usable oil from oil shale and shale oil worldwide is only 96 billion barrels. So even if we could wave our magic wands and get all that oil at once, at current world consumption rates, we would only have enough to meet the demand for a measly three years.

On top of all that, it's possible that extracting the amount needed to meet demand will never be economically feasible, and almost certainly not at current oil prices. All of this ignores the pressure from environmentalists concerned about the damage the extraction process can cause as well.

So yes, it is interesting that the United States holds such a large share of the world's supply of shale oil sources. But no, it's not going to do much to help the world stave off peak oil.

Peak Oil: Further Proof

The sad and frightening reality of peak oil is that it's already happened here at home, even with the short-term boost we will receive from shale oil. You might think it's impossible to make such a claim. You might find it difficult to believe that it's even possible to predict something as vast, fluid, and changing as domestic oil production. But here's my projection to the contrary, based on the information I've just shared.

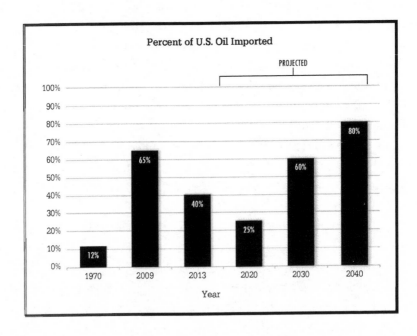

Notice the rapid increase in imported oil between 1970 and 2009. More alarmingly, notice the sharp decrease in imported oil between 2009 and 2013. Then also notice the reduction from 2013 to 2020. Those reductions don't derive from the fact that we suddenly don't need that oil. It's because of the short-term boost in US oil supply from shale oil production.

The chart shows a projection that US oil imports will go from 25% of usage in 2020 to 60% of usage in 2030 and 80% of usage in 2040. Why? First, conventional oil (which, again, is oil obtained by wells that drill directly into pools of oil), is declining in many wells in the world at a rate of up to 6% per year. New discoveries of conventional oil in the United States are minimal too. Conventional drilling offshore is becoming more expensive and hazardous. The recent BP disaster is an example.[29]

Second, the production of shale oil will be far less than currently anticipated, for all the reasons mentioned in the previous section.

Third, technical, environmental, water, energy use, political, and economic issues will derail any chance of production of oil from the kerogen in oil shale rock. When that short-term boost from shale oil ends and conventional oil reserves are nearly depleted, we'll be right back up on imports—even higher than we were before, with no reasonable possibility that we will ever again see a decrease.

Fourth, it's not the stated reserves themselves that matter, as no one uses the same rules in estimating them; it's how much oil can actually be produced that counts. For instance, recent reports suggest that the reserves in the tar sands in Canada (which we've known about for over 50 years), the reserves discovered five to seven miles deep off the shore of Brazil, or the reserves of shale oil and oil shale in the United States are all promising new discoveries with vast potential, but the problem is that a limited amount of this oil can be produced in a cost-effective and environmentally acceptable way.

The OPEC Cartel

I suspect that some of my readers might be wondering how new oil production in the world would change the price of oil. Good question, simple answer: even with new oil production, the price for oil would change very little. This is because the world price for a barrel of oil is set not solely by supply and demand or by the amount of money it costs to extract oil out of the ground.

If those were the only factors, then oil would cost just a low multiple of the $5 per barrel required to get oil out of the ground in Saudi Arabia and other OPEC countries.[30] Instead, over the past decade-plus, we have seen prices consistently hovering around $100 per barrel. Then, very recently, OPEC decided to let oil prices stay low in an effort to maintain their market share by making it difficult for other entities, including US shale oil drillers, to maintain their current levels of production.

These are just a couple of examples of how the OPEC cartel has enormous power to set the price. It derives this power in part from the fact that its members control 73% of global oil reserves and in part from the fact that they're backed by trillions of dollars of capital to sustain themselves whenever world oil prices get low. This control will only increase as other nations further decline in oil production. The commodity is so globalized— and so heavily controlled by one particular, unfailingly powerful entity— that the oil production of an individual non-OPEC country will have little impact on the long-term price of oil. Shale oil may alter this dynamic for a few years, but then we'll be right back to OPEC raising the price of oil.

OPEC can generally set the global price per barrel by controlling their production levels. Excepting the slight advantage of lower shipping costs at home, all US oil accomplishes is to add minimally to the total supply of oil worldwide. Of course, as long as the government refuses to let US oil be exported in a few years of plenty, US oil and gasoline prices could decline.

In any case, the impact of laboriously making oil out of rock that contains kerogen in the United States, as compared to the ease of filling up barrels of sweet crude in OPEC countries, is akin to the impact of a high school football team playing the Super Bowl champions. OPEC, just as they have done recently, could easily counter any increased production in global shale oil by simply dropping their own production, keeping world prices right where OPEC wants them to be. No matter what we do to increase our own oil production, in the long run, US and global oil prices will remain hostage to the profit-maximizing actions of OPEC.

World Oil Reserves

For those who still doubt the power of OPEC, let's take a look at where the oil reserves are allocated on the global stage. The chart below shows the top

15 countries in terms of percentage of remaining global oil reserves.[31] As you can see, OPEC members dominate the list.

15 Countries with the Largest Oil Reserves (2015)			
	RESERVES (billions of barrels)	SHARE OF WORLD OIL RESERVES	OIL ORTHODOXY
Venezuela	298.3	18.0%	OPEC
Saudi Arabia	265.8	16.0%	OPEC
Iran	172.5	10.4%	OPEC
Canada	157.8	9.5%	NON-OPEC
Iraq	144.2	8.7%	OPEC
Kuwait	101.5	6.1%	OPEC
United Arab Emirates	97.8	5.9%	OPEC
Russia	80.0	4.8%	NON-OPEC
Libya	48.4	2.9%	OPEC
United States	37.9	2.2%	NON-OPEC
Kazakhstan	30.0	1.8%	NON-OPEC
Nigeria	37.1	1.8%	OPEC
Qatar	25.2	1.5%	OPEC
China	24.6	1.5%	NON-OPEC
Brazil	15.3	0.9%	NON-OPEC
Top 15	1536.4	92.7%	

While the information in the chart above shows the US holding 2.2% of world oil reserves, my own research shows that a more realistic estimate includes the contributions from shale oil (which, as I mentioned earlier, is 24 billion barrels). So if we include shale oil, the percentage of US oil reserves moves up to 3.6%. To make matters simpler still, I'm going to round that number up to 4% in further discussion of US oil reserves.

Moving on, when we break it down to just OPEC countries versus the rest of the world, the picture is even more dramatic. Take a look at the chart below.[32]

OPEC vs. NON-OPEC Oil & Population (2014)				
	COUNTRIES	OIL RESERVES	POPULATION	% OF WORLD POP.
OPEC	12	73%	450,000,000	6%
NON-OPEC	184	27%	6,550,000,000	94%

The next startling geopolitical reality comes when you compare US reserves to the reserves of the rest of the world. The pie looks like this:[33]

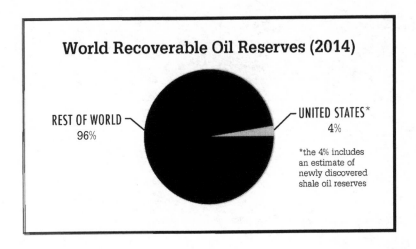

As I mentioned, that's my shale-oil-boosted and rounded-up percentage for US oil reserves, and we're still looking at a mere 4% of world oil reserves controlled by the United States. To be in such a situation is actually a bit frightening economically, knowing that several of the OPEC nations listed above are not exactly on friendly terms with the United States.

Added to the possible severe economic disruption from peak oil is the apparent fact that perhaps most of the oil-producing countries in the world are in the same boat as the United States. Projections suggest that if they haven't reached conventional peak oil already, they will reach it relatively soon.[34]

Peak Oil Reached (2013)			
Algeria	Guinea	Norway	Tunisia
Argentina	Indonesia	Oman	United Kingdom
Australia	Iran	Peru	United States
Brunei	Iraq	Romania	Uzbekistan
Chad	Kuwait	Russia	Venezuela
Denmark	Libya	Sudan	Vietnam
Egypt	Malaysia	Syria	Yemen
Gabon	Mexico	Trinidad & Tobago	

Peak Oil Not Yet Reached (2013)			
Angola	Colombia	Kazakhstan	Thailand
Azerbaijan	Congo	Nigeria	Turkmenistan
Brazil	Ecuador	Qatar	United Arab Emirates
Canada	India	Saudi Arabia	
China	Italy		

The tables above show that, of the world's oil-producing countries, 35 have already reached peak oil—and many of them reached it long ago, just like the United States did in 1970.[35] The average date the countries above reached peak oil and started their rapid decline in production was 1995. That leaves 14 countries that have yet to reach peak oil. And of those 14 countries, many are near their peak.

So in summary, all the charts I've thrown at you mean five things for the world.

1. Total oil production will reach peak and decline, driving oil prices skyward.
2. Oil reserves lie overwhelmingly within OPEC countries.
3. Conventional oil has already peaked, and new discoveries will be limited.
4. Shale oil is predicted to peak in 2016 for the US and will peak later on for the world as a whole.[36]
5. The United States will have severe trouble meeting its huge demand long term with its soon-to-be-dwindling supply.

Global Population versus Global Oil Use

First off, let's get one important reality out of the way. The following charts show that, while the United States represents only 5% of the world's population, it consumes 20% of the world's oil.[37]

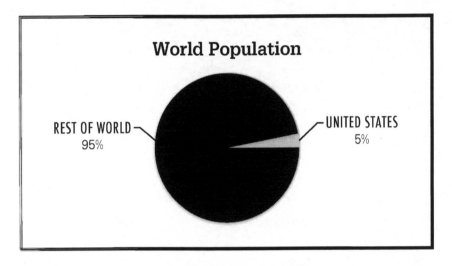

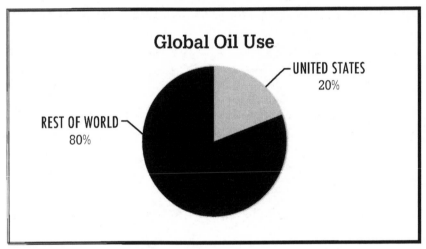

What this means is that there is absolutely no way the US can become independent of OPEC-controlled oil long term. 20% of world oil consumed versus holding a measly 4% of the world's oil reserves? Let me put it this way: if a person thinks the US will become permanently oil independent with those numbers so far out of whack, that person is one sandwich short of a picnic.

Global economic trends show that many countries are on a rapid-paced track toward developed status as well, which means there will be even *less* oil to go around. As these many countries move toward the US standard of living, oil demand will rise to the point that it overwhelms oil supply.

It doesn't take a Nobel Prize winner to figure out what will happen to the price then.

Of those many emerging countries, let's consider the numbers we can expect from just one: China. China is home to 1.2 billion people, or about four times the population of the United States. We know that the United States currently uses about 20% of the world's oil supply. So if China were to live and drive as we do here in the United States, it would consume 80% of the oil produced in the world every year. Only 20% of world production would be available for all the other 194 countries, the United States included.

This is a simplified argument, of course, but I'm also simplifying the projection of worldwide growth in GDP. Even if we assume that the world will produce enough additional oil to meet China's demand, there are still 194 other countries to consider. It's easy to see that, whatever the supply, it will not be enough to provide the world with a US standard of living, or even anything close.

What do you suppose a continually increasing world demand and declining production will do to the cost of a barrel of oil? Probably this:

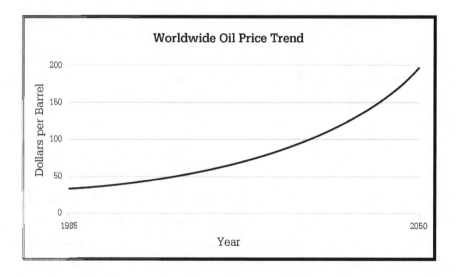

Even a conservative estimate puts us at a significant price increase in the long term. So even though gas prices are low currently and likely to remain so for a few years, at some point, you're looking at five-dollar-per-gallon gas (or even higher). If we see a significant disruption in the Middle East coupled with peak oil, who knows how high the price could go? It could be devastating for the world economy.

Ethanol Will Fill the New Demand for Fuel

It seems logical to suggest that emerging countries, along with the United States, will have to find new ways to meet the demand—ways that are as cheap and efficient as possible. By now, it should be quite clear that there is only one alternative to gasoline, only one fuel source that can power those two billion ICEs people will own in 2030: ethanol. Only ethanol realistically stands in a position to fill the gap between supply of fuel and demand for fuel.

Since ICEs aren't going away, but gasoline gradually is, we can draw the conclusion that the world will need to move in a direction that allows it to meet the increasing demand for fuel for cars. How will it do that? By creating as much ethanol as possible. To meet the demand demonstrated above, the world will have to go from producing the 23 billion gallons of ethanol per year it currently makes[38] to 180 billion gallons in 2040.

But how could we possibly generate that much ethanol in a given year? One way would be by growing as much corn as possible. But isn't corn expensive? And is it even possible to grow that much corn?

Corn Prices Will Come Down

Corn prices move up and down, sometimes dramatically, according to how much corn is harvested relative to consumer demand. For example, in 2012, the price per bushel of corn soared from $3.50 to over $7.00.[39] Why? A lower supply of corn due to the most severe drought in 50 years. By 2015, a year where the corn crop production was normal, the price was back down to $3.60 per bushel. Past spikes in corn prices were almost always the result of a drop in the amount of corn planted compared to the previous year. One exception was 2008, when the increase in price was due largely to the most excessive speculation in the corn market in modern times.

But the main reason corn prices fluctuate is that farmers tend to have different planting habits from year to year. When prices are high in one year, farmers are compelled to plant more corn so they can make more money. This causes the price for corn to drop. Then, in the next year, the lower prices for corn compel farmers not to plant as much corn, which causes corn prices to rise. The cycle simply reflects a supply change created by the farmers. If demand stays about the same each year, a low amount planted results in higher prices, while a high amount planted results in lower prices. Supply and demand. Simple.

Further, the price of US corn, like that of US oil, is to some extent set by *global* supply and demand, not just domestic supply and demand. This is important to point out because it has become clear that other nations are now growing and exporting more corn than before. Brazil and Argentina, for example, have recently increased their exports.[40] This is a good thing for the global price of corn, as more supply will drive prices down.

Corn Yield per Acre Is Increasing

The graph below shows the steep upward trajectory of annual yields of US corn since 1926:[41]

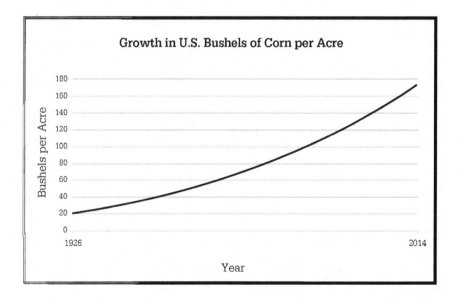

The crux of why you see that tremendous upward trajectory is that the past 80-plus years have seen remarkable advances in agriculture and corn production technology.[42] With these factors at play, we can project continued increases in corn supply.

Truly the only limit to the amount of corn we can grow worldwide is the land itself, and that limit could be expanded considerably in the coming years because the technology for growing corn can be transferred to many places on the planet. Additionally, corn seed companies are developing corn that is resistant to drought, which helps improve the outlook.

Currently, the United States produces approximately 13 billion bushels of corn per year, which is 40% of the world production of 32 billion bushels.[43] The United States accomplishes this feat because it is capable of producing, on average, at least 160 bushels of corn per acre of land, while the rest of the corn-producing world lags behind.

One example of a lagging country is China. It is the world's second-largest producer of corn after the United States, yet its corn yield, at 90 bushels per acre, is well below the American standard.

But China and other countries outside the United States won't lag for long. The average for all corn-producing countries in the world is about 76 bushels per acre.[44] If other countries employ the same advances in corn and agricultural technology that we have seen in the US, they will eventually produce more corn per acre and at some point may produce as much per acre as the United States does now.

That's not even the half of it. Given the latest advancements in seed, fertilizer, and cultivation technology (as reported by the leading genetically engineered corn seed companies in the world, Monsanto, Syngenta, and Pioneer Hi-Bred), any country that wants to get into the corn-producing business could one day be capable of producing 300 bushels per acre.[45] This is not a dream, by the way. In 2014, a farmer in Georgia grew the record crop with 503 bushels per acre. The 18 farmers that finished just behind him averaged 383 bushels per acre. If and when that reality comes to pass for the average farmer, it would double total US production from 13 billion bushels to 26 billion bushels *without using any additional land.*

The bottom line is that it seems entirely realistic to believe that world corn yield could increase sharply. This is how such an increase in production would look:

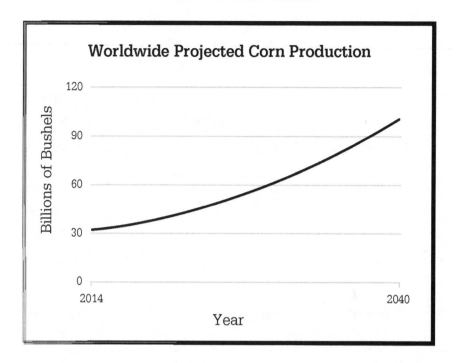

Worldwide Projected Corn Production

The world already knows where and how to grow 96 billion bushels of corn. The reason the increased production is not occurring is that no one is currently willing to pay enough for the corn. But once demand for ethanol soars, the money will be there, and the corn will be grown.

"So what?" you might say. "If we grow more corn, we won't just need it for ethanol. We'll need it for food and animal feed."

True. Let's examine that idea.

In the United States, we use about 40% of our annual corn crop for ethanol production. My data shows that, in 2040, the world will see a demand of 180 billion gallons of ethanol per year.

Worldwide Production of Gasoline & Ethanol	2014 ACTUAL	2040 PROJECTED
Gasoline Production (gallons)	300 billion	300 billion
Ethanol Production (gallons)	23 billion	180 billion
Total Production (gallons)	323 billion	480 billion

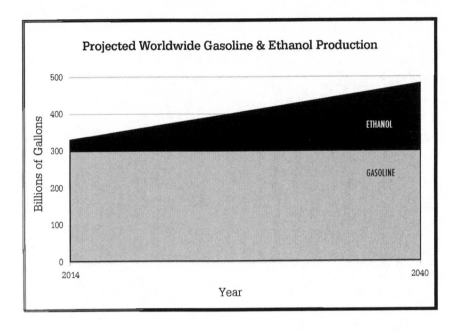

Projected Worldwide Gasoline & Ethanol Production

Knowing what we know about the coming increase in corn crop production, we also know that we will require approximately 40% of the global supply of corn to meet the future global demand for ethanol. We're looking at an equal share of 40% of United States corn and 40% of world corn in order to meet the demand, by the way. That leaves the other 60% of each left over for food and feed.

I've been simplifying the argument a little because there is more than one way to produce ethanol. You don't necessarily have to use corn. In fact, 30% of the ethanol now produced in the world is derived from sugarcane in Brazil and a few other countries. That's not a crop we currently grow for ethanol in the United States, but in some southern areas of the country we could do so, and we should begin to do so. It certainly works well in Brazil. Technological and agricultural innovations, as well as an increase in land use for the crop, are also increasing the yield from sugarcane in that country. You might also notice in the chart below that I have labeled 10% of ethanol production as "other." This acknowledges the 10% of ethanol produced in several other countries that have recently begun using a wide variety of feedstocks to create ethanol, including wheat, barley, sugar beets, sweet sorghum, rapeseed, and sweet potatoes.[46]

If the technology for both corn and sugarcane were applied in other parts of the world, here is what the contribution breakdown for each crop could look like in the future:

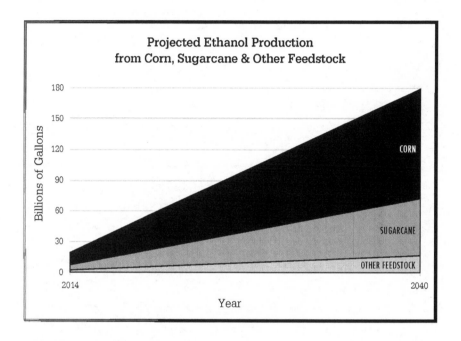

Out of 23 billion gallons of ethanol made worldwide, the United States generates about 60% of the total. Meanwhile, Brazil makes about 6.3 billion gallons from sugarcane for approximately 27% of the world total.[47] Several other nations, using a variety of corn, sugarcane, and other feedstocks, make up the other 13%.

If we keep these proportions similar, we won't need to use corn alone to meet the projected future demand of 180 billion gallons of ethanol in 2040. About 101 billion gallons would come from corn ethanol. About 49 billion gallons would come from sugarcane. The other 30 billion gallons would come from the other feedstocks used in other ethanol-producing countries.

While it's possible that cellulosic ethanol, which is made from plant material and wood, will add some to the above totals, that technology remains largely in the experimental stage (with a few notable exceptions, such as the commercially successful processing of corn waste into cellulosic ethanol by Poet, Inc. of the US, the world's largest producer of ethanol).

Whether or not the near future brings us any major breakthroughs in cellulosic ethanol, the US would do well to continue supporting research and development.

Distillers Grain—Additional Food for Animals

As an aside, let me address an important point. Many opponents of ethanol suggest that the more corn we use for fuel, the more expensive corn will become. If we make corn so expensive, it will be more expensive for farmers to feed their cattle and other animals. If we make it more expensive for farmers to feed their animals, then we also make it more expensive for the consumer to buy a steak.

Well, as is the case for most misguided arguments, the people who think this way aren't seeing the whole picture. When you produce ethanol, you're not actually converting into ethanol the entirety of the corn you use. After the starch in the corn becomes ethanol, the remainder of the corn kernel can be found suspended in a watery mass called *stillage*. This is the primary byproduct of ethanol production. If you filter the water out of the stillage, you're left with what's called *distillers grain*, which is a high-protein feed that can be consumed by cattle and other farm animals. Interestingly, distillers grain is actually preferable to raw corn because it is comparatively higher in protein.

What this means is that the parts of the corn left over from the ethanol distilling process can be used to feed animals. In fact, we can reintroduce about 30% of the corn used for ethanol into the pool of corn used for feed. "Roughly one third of every 56-pound bushel of grain that enters the ethanol process is enhanced and returned to the animal feed market, mostly in the form of distillers grains, corn gluten feed, and gluten meal."[48] In other words, this byproduct of ethanol production is a valuable commodity. Farmers can feed distillers grain to animals either wet or dry. Since the feed is preferable to standard corn, the demand for it is tremendously high. Plus, if distillers grain is dried, it can be shipped worldwide. That's happening right now and will continue to happen in the future, no matter where we go with ethanol production.

For the more technically minded and data-oriented of my readers, allow me to break it down briefly. The important thing is this: ethanol production uses about 40% of the field corn grown in the United States. I project that percentage to be the same worldwide by 2030. Of that amount of corn used for ethanol, about 30% comes out in the form of distillers grain, which we can reintroduce to the total stock of corn used for feed. This means that the net use of corn for ethanol is not 40% of the crop, but rather only 28%. Therefore, the net total corn crop used to make ethanol is twelve percentage points less than is almost always stated in the media. The equivalent of 72% of the total corn crop, not just 60%, can be used for feeding cattle and other animals.[49]

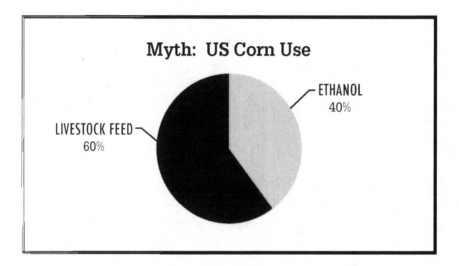

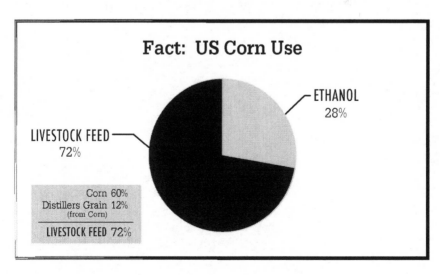

Conclusion

I have shared many things with you in this chapter, so let's summarize.

The internal combustion engine will continue to meet at least 90% of global demand for cars for many years to come. While that's happening, global demand for cars will double to two billion by 2030. To fuel those two billion cars, we will need an estimated 480 billion gallons of fuel per year.

The world is now producing 300 billion gallons of gasoline per year, and we'll never produce more than that. So where are we going to get those extra 180 billion gallons of fuel we'll eventually need? We can only get it from one source: ethanol.

There is good news in all this. Ethanol can and will get the job done. Oil production will decline and ultimately run out entirely. Corn prices will remain competitive in the long run—in fact, future projections paint a rather rosy picture for the supply of corn. The world will eventually find itself capable of producing more than double the amount of corn it currently produces.

The longer-term future holds twice the cars, much less oil, and substantially more corn. This means that ethanol will become the lowest-cost fuel for the internal combustion engine, which in turn means that Team Ethanol will be in prime position to win the Fuel Conference.

Ethanol in Depth

Team Ethanol's success depends on many factors. Among them are production, distribution, and use; economic viability; government policy; environmental impact; ethanol byproducts; and advancements in the science of ethanol production. In this chapter, I'll briefly examine them all. In this way, I'll further cement the case that Team Ethanol beats Team Gasoline at every turn.

But before we get into the specifics, let's consider the premises for my argument that ethanol has the potential for economic superiority.

As we all know, gasoline is made out of oil, which is a nonrenewable resource. This is why the price will someday be much, much higher than it is now.

Meanwhile, ethanol is made out of the raw material of corn, sugarcane, or plant waste material, all of which are renewable resources. All one has to do to keep the price of ethanol lower than that of gasoline is to produce a large enough amount of the raw material. It's possible to keep that price reasonable because there is an enormous additional amount of land on which the raw material for ethanol can be grown. Plus, biotechnological advances are making it possible to grow greater and greater amounts of corn and sugarcane per acre.

A car's engine can be made to run on 100% ethanol. This means that, whenever we so choose, we will no longer have to include expensive gasoline in the mix of ethanol that we have in circulation today (where the ethanol in the mix ranges from 10% to as high as 85%, with the balance being gasoline).

All these factors combine to mean that, as the cost of gasoline soars at some point in the future, the price of ethanol will be much lower than that of gasoline. Contest over. Ethanol wins. It's only a matter of time.

But just in case that picture isn't quite enough to convince you, consider some of the other factors that play to Team Ethanol's advantage.

Gasoline Contains Benzene and Other Air Pollutants

Gasoline is bad for you in more ways than one. It doesn't just impact your wallet; it impacts your health. *Greatly*. It's so bad for your health, in fact, that if gasoline were a brand new product (one that hadn't been in circulation all over the world for decades), it's hard to imagine that the EPA, WHO, or FDA would allow companies to make and sell it to the public. Products this dangerous don't often get the clearance to hit the market anymore.

Ignoring the health risk for a moment, gasoline is plain terrible for the environment. With regard to global warming, gasoline has 59% *more* greenhouse gas compared to ethanol.[1] This disparity is so huge that, if all cars in the United States ran strictly on ethanol, it would be like removing 3.5 million vehicles from the roads.[2]

But what I would like to focus on in this section is the other, less often discussed advantage of ethanol exhaust over gasoline exhaust. While it is true that both exhausts contain noxious fumes like nitrous oxide and carbon monoxide, gasoline's exhaust contains substantially higher amounts of a particularly damaging agent: benzene.[3]

Studies have shown that a person exposed to benzene in the air has a greater chance of experiencing the following health problems: anemia, preleukemia, nucleated red blood cells, decreases in hemoglobin, granular lymphocytes, myeloid dysplasia, abnormal platelets, and myelofibrosis. Researchers are now studying the possibility that auto exhaust may negatively impact the brain regions responsible for behavior, personality, and decision making. Studies are also underway regarding the impact of exhaust on the genes of a newborn baby; possible increased risk of developing Alzheimer's disease or Parkinson's disease; reduction in the IQ of children who are heavily exposed to exhaust; and the likelihood that such children would suffer from anxiety, depression, and attention disorders.[4]

It's well known that many diseases have partially genetic causes, and research into the human genome has recently determined that some people have genes that predispose them to cancer. The key word is *predispose*. A possible implication is that someone can be genetically susceptible to developing cancer, but that person won't necessarily develop cancer unless he or she encounters something in his or her environment that "flips the switch." So even someone with a genetic predisposition to cancer can go a lifetime without contracting the disease—just so long as he or she avoids encountering high doses of cancer-causing agents, commonly called *carcinogens.*

Why have we raised benzene as important? Because it's a known carcinogen.

Imagine all those cars fueled with 100% gasoline driving America's roadways. They're all pumping a cancer-causing agent into the air we breathe. Could this be a contributing factor to the steep upswing in the occurrence of cancer over the past century?[5] And if we switched our cars to ethanol, which contains no benzene, could that trend be at least partially reversed?

The Real Cost of Gasoline

Many opponents of ethanol suggest that it's not a viable product because you need so much federal and state government subsidy for ethanol. While that has been true in the past, it's simply not the case anymore. Ethanol production plants no longer receive direct subsidy payments.[6]

The loudest opponents of Team Ethanol often reside in the Team Gasoline camp, which is why it's so interesting that they frequently crow about the subsidy-for-ethanol non-issue mentioned above. Here's a startling fact: The government pours a staggering amount of subsidy into the production of gasoline. Estimates suggest that Big Oil receives a full $2.50 subsidy for every gallon of gasoline it produces. Consider the following list of tax subsidies given directly to the oil industry:[7]

Oil Industry: Tax Subsidies	
Foreign Tax Credit	Fuel Production Credit
Oil Recovery Credit	Foreign Income Deferral
Depletion Allowance	Expensing of Exploration Cost
State Tax Credit	Export Financing Subsidy
Development Subsidy	Accelerated Depreciation Allowances
State/Local Tax Reduction	Tax Payer Relief Act of 1997

And that doesn't even include all the money we're spending on military matters as we protect oil-rich countries. Why did we intervene in Iraq? Weapons of mass destruction? Well, we might have used that as justification to start the war, but once we knew the weapons weren't there, why didn't we just come home? Because we wanted to depose a tyrannical dictator? Possibly, but weren't there at least a few more tyrannical dictators in the world in greater need of deposing? To free a people from oppression? Surely there must have been people in the world who were worse off than in Iraq.[*] Did we pick a country at random to change into a democracy because we want to establish democracies around the world? It doesn't seem likely. So why, then, did we really wage war in Iraq?

No matter how you look at it, the logical answer has to be oil. We invaded because it was an oil-rich country that we wanted to stabilize and use as a buffer of US influence in the center of the largest oil supply in the world. We stayed there for many years in an attempt to improve our access to world oil reserves and to have some influence over the price of oil.

Maybe you don't agree with me. But just for fun, let's assume the war in Iraq was about oil. If we do so, we have to think about how much that war for oil cost us and then add that cost to the total cost to produce a gallon of gasoline. During periods when there is no war, the estimated annual cost of the *oil defense subsidy* (the cost to have military in place to protect our oil supply) is $96 billion. If we add on the actual cost of the war in Iraq ($757 billion for ongoing military matters and $1 trillion for healthcare and direct benefits for Iraq War veterans after the war), the total is easily over two trillion dollars.[8]

And as long as we're talking about things that cost the taxpayers a great deal of money, we might as well discuss damage from oil spills. When you spill a tanker of oil in the ocean, it kills the wildlife and devastates the ecosystem. This is why Team Ethanol enjoys such a strong advantage in this department: when you spill a tanker of ethanol into the ocean it evaporates, and the only environmental impact is a few drunken fish. The cost for cleanup is therefore zero.

So if we consider all that tax revenue lost in needless subsidies for oil and oil protection expenses, we have to recognize that we're actually paying a whole lot more than $3.50 for a gallon of gasoline. Sure, that's all we're paying at the pump; but we're paying for gas again every April 15 when it comes time to send in the tax returns. Adding up just the subsidies, we're looking at $6.00 per gallon of gas. And if we can assume the war in Iraq is

---

[*] More than a few countries in Africa come to mind.

about oil, then you've got to tack on the cost of the war as well. That puts the real price to the taxpayer somewhere between $8.00 and $9.00 per gallon.

Meanwhile, it currently costs about $2.50 to produce a gallon of ethanol, and that's without *any* direct subsidy. The cost to the taxpayer to buy a gallon of ethanol at the time of this writing is approximately $2.75. So if we assume a consumer price of $2.75 per gallon of ethanol, and we compare it to the real cost of gasoline, which is $6.00 per gallon on the low end and $9.00 per gallon on the high end, this one seems like a no-brainer. The government should support ethanol, not oil and gasoline.

In terms of the political landscape, the picture seems even clearer. What if we could produce all the fuel for all our cars right here in the United States? Wouldn't it cost substantially less? Yes. Wouldn't the government need to dole out far less subsidy to the gasoline industry? Yes. Wouldn't we retain $300 billion for the United States rather than sending it overseas? Yes. And as that $300 billion circulated through the economy, wouldn't it add to our economic growth? Yes. Wouldn't it stop us from fighting overseas wars for oil? Yes. And perhaps the most important underlying factor: wouldn't converting to ethanol as our primary fuel create thousands of new American jobs? Yes.

As you can see in the chart below, there are many benefits to the use of ethanol in the United States. The government receives an additional $8.6 billion per year in tax revenues; government farm program payments to farmers are reduced by $10.1 billion per year; gasoline consumers save an estimated $34.5 billion per year; and the ethanol industry enlarges the US GDP by $53.6 billion per year.[9]

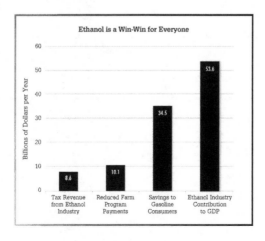

This seems pretty straightforward. We can keep paying subsidies to oil companies and fighting wars to protect our supply of imported oil and pay the real cost of $6.00 to $9.00 per gallon of gasoline, or we can stop spending money for those things and use it for better purposes—perhaps education, infrastructure, research, job training, and other programs that build for the future. On top of all that, we can prosper from the job creation, cleaner and healthier air, and huge contribution to the economy that ethanol promises.

Production and Distribution of Ethanol

Below is a simplified schematic of how ethanol is produced.[10] Basically, corn kernels are ground up and put through fermentation, and the result is a pure alcohol (technically ethyl alcohol) called ethanol.

As I mentioned in the previous chapter, the parts of the corn left over from the ethanol production process are called distillers grain, which can be used to feed animals. Exports of both ethanol and distillers grains are currently booming.

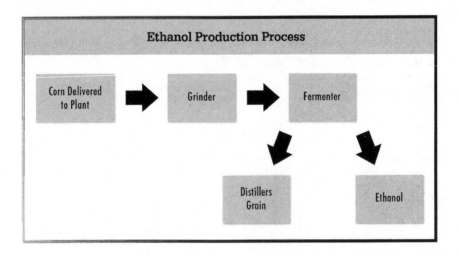

To illustrate what the above process looks like in the real world, here is a picture of an ethanol plant:

When trucks deliver raw corn to the ethanol plant above, that corn gets stored in the corn storage bin (1). Ethanol plants like these will keep plenty of stored corn on hand in case of bad weather preventing new corn deliveries. The rectangular building (2) is where machinery grinds the corn, feeds it into a fermenter, and then separates the resultant materials into ethanol and distillers grain. That exhaust stack (3) you see is releasing nothing more than steam from the water used in the ethanol-making process.** The round structure (5) is the ethanol holding tank, which is where the plant stores the ethanol. In the foreground you see a series of railroad tanker cars (4), each of them capable of transporting up to 30,000 gallons of ethanol.

At present, the United States produces approximately 13 billion gallons of fuel ethanol per year, compared to the approximately 128 billion gallons of gasoline it consumes.[11] That means that about 90% of the fuel Americans consume is gasoline and 10% is ethanol.

How does that work? The gas you put in your tank is actually E10, which is a mixture of 90% gasoline and 10% ethanol. So the next time somebody asks you, "Where can I buy some ethanol?" be sure to answer, "You're already buying it." It's in the gas you put in your car. The better question is, how much gasoline can we replace with ethanol?

** Ethanol plants are extraordinarily environmentally friendly. The water used in the ethanol-making process leaves the plant as part of the ethanol, as moisture in distillers grain, as clean steam through the exhaust stack, is recycled, or occasionally drained off into a holding pool from which it slowly evaporates.

The EPA recently approved E15 to replace E10. So eventually we'll be going from 10% ethanol in every gallon of ICE fuel to 15%.[12] Put simply, this means a demand for 50% more ethanol, or 6 billion gallons, which will require the building of approximately 60 new hundred-million-gallon-per-year ethanol plants.

In addition to E15, we find a high-percentage-ethanol fuel on the other end of the spectrum. This one's called E85.*** It flips the script on the gasoline/ethanol ratio, checking in at 85% ethanol versus only 15% gasoline. This is the fuel used in the so-called flex-fuel cars.[13] A flex-fuel car can run on any mixture from 100% gasoline to 85% ethanol. At the time of this writing, 25% of the cars produced in the United States are flex-fuel cars. It costs about $400 to convert a car to a flex-fuel car with a few small changes in the fuel system. The change kit is available nationwide. When the price of gasoline soars in the coming years, and E85 remains far cheaper than gasoline, you might want to keep that in mind.

Once a plant produces the ethanol, it pumps it into 30,000-gallon liquid-container railcars or tanker trucks and sends it either directly to a gas station for use in a blender pump, to an oil/gasoline company to be blended into E10, or to ships bound for export.

Blender pumps are a remarkable invention, rather simple in design. Basically, these pumps feature one tank of pure ethanol and one tank of pure gasoline. They mix a ratio of gasoline and ethanol depending on the end user's needs. Here is what a blender pump looks like:

*** Why E85 and not E100 (as in fuel that is 100% ethanol)? Because 85% is the highest amount of ethanol on which the internal combustion engine is designed to run.

So if you want E85 for your car, you push the button that says "E85" and the pump mixes up some 85% ethanol and 15% gasoline for you. If the next guy in line wants E20, he presses the corresponding button and gets 80% gasoline and 20% ethanol. Additional mixes of ethanol available include E10, E20, E30, E40, or E85. Magical.

The Ethanol Economic Model

Suppose there were two drug companies that had a shared patent on a particular drug. This means these two companies are the only ones in the country that can sell this drug. Let's call them Company A and Company B.

Now, suppose the drug we're talking about is important. Let's say that everyone has to take it in order to drive their cars every day. If you don't take this pill, you have to ride the bus to work. As you can imagine, demand for this drug would be extremely high.

Then suppose our two companies owned two different pieces of land from which the materials for this drug could be extracted. These are the only two pieces of land on the planet from which this drug can be produced. And suppose that, for whatever reason, it becomes much more difficult to extract the drug from one of the sites than the other. For this reason, the drug produced by Company A now costs double the price of the drug produced by Company B.

Given these factors, what share of the market would Company B control? The answer is that Company B, with its much lower production costs, could price its drug just under the break-even price of Company A. Company B would therefore have a huge economic advantage, and in time, it would control virtually 100% of the market.

This is exactly the case with ethanol and gasoline. Company A, with the much higher production cost, is gasoline, and Company B, with the lower production cost, is ethanol. As with the drugs, once gasoline soars in price, ethanol can set a selling price well below that of gasoline. Therefore, as the gasoline price increases, and the corn price stays reasonable, ethanol is on its way to enormous demand with a higher and higher percentage of sales versus gasoline in the fuel market.

What this means is that ethanol will have a tremendous competitive advantage. It's a renewable resource, its supply exists (and will continue to exist) in low-cost abundance, and the demand for it will rise in the years to come. Meanwhile, its chief competition will have to scramble to keep up its supply over the next 20 years and beyond.

Effectively, the business model for ethanol is a bit like the business model for a monopoly. It's currently one of only two games in town. But every year after peak oil hits, as the number of ICEs continues to grow, it will inch closer to being the *only* game in town.

Surely there must be something that could go wrong with this rosy outlook for ethanol? Yes. There are two things, in fact.

First, corn prices could become too high relative to the price per gallon of ethanol. The previous chapter demonstrated at length why corn prices will not increase continuously, but allow me to reiterate here:

1. Corn is a renewable commodity, and the amount planted each year could be set based on demand considerations.
2. New seed genetics and advancements in agricultural technology are expected to double the yield per acre over the next 20 years.
3. The planet has an additional one billion acres[14] of unused crop land. Some of that could be used to grow corn (and this is *without* encroaching on the rainforest or any other fragile land). So it is entirely reasonable to expect that we will one day expand into unused agricultural land to meet the demand for more corn.

The second factor that could disrupt economically feasible ethanol production is a large supply of ethanol relative to demand, but this is an improbable scenario to imagine, because projections place long-term demand at 180 billion gallons per year, compared to the approximately 23 billion gallons currently produced. Supplying that additional 157 billion gallons would require the construction of 1,570 new 100-million-gallon ethanol plants in the world.

Ethanol Is a High-Performance Fuel

There are a number of rumors regarding ethanol's expected level of performance in terms of horsepower and engine heat. Opponents of ethanol would like you to believe that if you fill your tank with ethanol, you can kiss your car's high-level performance goodbye. You'll lose horsepower. Your engine will overheat. You'll wind up with engine gunk. Your valves will burn out. In the winter, your fuel lines will freeze. It's all false, of course. Just ask the Indianapolis 500 and NASCAR racing series whether ethanol is a high-performance, clean-burning fuel.

Indy 500 cars have 650-horsepower engines that propel them at an average speed of 220 mph.[15] For a car like this, performance is everything. So if ethanol is so much worse in terms of a car's performance, why have the reviews been so high following the series' recent switch to a fuel composed of pure ethanol?

Meanwhile, NASCAR has switched from standard gasoline to E15, a fuel containing 15% ethanol. The reason behind the switch was an attempt to burn a greener fuel, and one that supported American jobs (the E15 used on this circuit is produced from corn grown exclusively in the United States). After months of racing with the new fuel, reports have come back that the green and job-saving initiative led to an unexpected benefit: the cars are actually achieving *more* horsepower. The NASCAR series has been so happy with the change that it recently surpassed its three millionth mile on E15.[16] That's a whole lot of miles to drive high-performance cars on a supposedly lower-performance fuel.

So the next time someone tells you that ethanol will rob your engine of performance, tell that person that if it's good enough for professional race car drivers, it's good enough for you.

Worldwide Use of Ethanol

Back in 2003, there were only 13 developed countries in the world that had any interest in using or producing the fuel, with the top three being the United States, Brazil, and Sweden. As one of the pioneering countries, Sweden imported ethanol from Brazil and then employed the effective countrywide distribution system they had developed for use of ethanol in cars.

Today, every country with a substantial number of vehicles is interested in the production or use of ethanol. And how far we've come in a decade! In 2003, there were only 13 countries producing and/or importing ethanol. Now there are 116. Amazing progress for Team Ethanol.

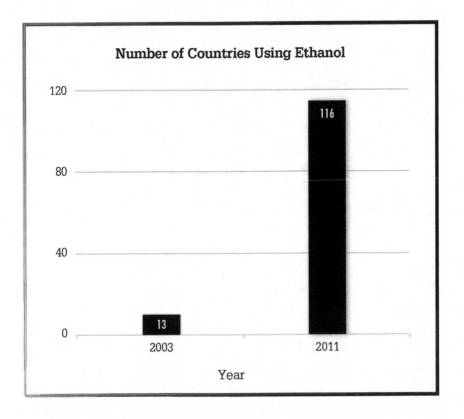

Below, you will find all 116 countries listed by name. Note that several of the countries are shaded. These are the countries that were involved in ethanol as early as 2003. The nonshaded countries have become involved in ethanol since 2003. In this way, you can see the vast increase in ethanol usage throughout the world.

Countries Using Ethanol in 2011 (2003 Countries Shaded)

Angola	Dominican Republic	Madagascar	Singapore
Argentina	Ecuador	Malawi	Slovakia
Armenia	Egypt	Malaysia	Slovenia
Australia	El Salvador	Mali	South Africa
Austria	Eritrea	Mauritius	South Korea
Azerbaijan	Estonia	Mexico	Spain
Bangladesh	Finland	Moldova	Sri Lanka
Barbados	France	Mozambique	Sudan
Belarus	Georgia	Netherlands	Suriname
Belgium	Germany	New Zealand	Sweden
Bolivia	Ghana	Nicaragua	Switzerland
Bosnia	Greece	Nigeria	Syria
Brazil	Guatemala	North Korea	Taiwan
Bulgaria	Guyana	Norway	Tanzania
Burkina Faso	Honduras	Oman	Thailand
Burundi	Hong Kong	Pakistan	Togo
Cameroon	Hungary	Panama	Trinidad/Tobago
Canada	India	Papua New Guinea	Turkey
Cape Verde	Israel	Peru	Turkmenistan
Chile	Italy	Philippines	Ukraine
China	Ivory Coast	Poland	United Arab Emirates
Colombia	Jamaica	Puerto Rico	United Kingdom
Congo	Japan	Reunion	United States
Costa Rica	Jordan	Romania	Uruguay
Croatia	Kenya	Russia	Venezuela
Cuba	Latvia	Rwanda	Yemen
Cyprus	Lithuania	Senegal	Zambia
Czech Republic	Macau	Serbia	Zimbabwe
Denmark	Macedonia	Sierra Leone	

China, India, Indonesia, Brazil, and other significant emerging-market countries will account for the bulk of the world's economic expansion over at least the next 25 years. That major economic expansion will mean that an overwhelming percentage of the additional billion cars we expect to see by 2030 will reside in developing countries.

As these countries grow their economies (currently, projections suggest some will grow their economies at a rate of six percent per year or more), the increase in cars and the demand for imported ethanol will soar. China is already producing more cars each year than the United States, and contrary to rumor and the media, 99% of these cars sport internal combustion engines. This means that there is plenty of opportunity for ethanol to become one of the chief exports for the United States.

US Exports of Ethanol

From 2000 to 2009, US exports of ethanol averaged 100 million gallons per year. From 2010 through 2014, exports jumped to an average of 750 million gallons per year. In 2014, ethanol was exported to 37 countries.[17]

What was the reason for the big jump from 100 million gallons to 750 million gallons? By 2010, the US had put in place many new overseas distribution channels and contracts for exporting ethanol (and there are more to come). Other factors pushing ethanol exports higher include: (1) the number of cars in the world is increasing by an estimated 50 million per year, (2) ethanol is cheaper than gasoline in the countries that are importing ethanol, and (3) 116 countries need that cheaper ethanol so their economies won't fall into recession due to high gasoline prices. With all of these factors, it's easy to see that the demand for ethanol from the United States will expand in the years to come—probably at a rapid rate.

The chart below shows the countries to which the United States already exports its ethanol. The point to take away from this chart is that, while the picture looks pretty already, it is only going to get better. Ethanol exports are high despite the fact that export channels are not yet fully developed. When they are developed, ethanol exports will go even higher. At the time of this writing, the United States is setting up the mechanisms and marketing channels to many more of the 116 countries in need of ethanol.[18]

Top 10 Importers of U.S. Ethanol (2010)			
Rank	Country	Total Ethanol	Percent of Total
1	Canada	119,446,063	30.1%
2	Netherlands	72,852,933	18.4%
3	United Kingdom	30,040,956	7.6%
4	India	28,873,148	7.3%
5	United Arab Emirates	28,529,896	7.2%
6	Brazil	22,649,389	5.7%
7	Jamaica	19,643,131	5.0%
8	Mexico	19,407,961	4.9%
9	Australia	9,101,874	2.3%
10	Nigeria	8,435,669	2.1%
	Rest of World	37,800,523	9.5%
	World Total	**396,781,543**	

Source: statistica.com

The United States produces more ethanol than any other country—60% of total world production. Once the export channels are fully operational and open, the US can begin exporting a higher percentage of the ethanol it produces. This will in turn alleviate recent concerns that the US has been producing *too much* of the fuel.**** Given growing world demand for ethanol and the establishment of export channels, any amount of ethanol surplus in the United States can easily be exported into world markets.

**** Recently, ethanol production was cited to have climbed above government mandate.

Ethanol Byproducts

One of the most interesting things about ethanol is that the process of creating it generates more than just tremendously effective and limitlessly renewable fuel. Even its byproducts can be used for the benefit of the world.

I've already mentioned distillers grain, but let me stress again that because of its higher protein content, this product is actually *preferable* to raw corn as animal feed. Every 56-pound bushel of corn used in the fermentation process generates about 2.8 gallons of ethanol and 17 pounds of distillers grain.[19] We know plenty about the value of ethanol, but distillers grain is a tremendously marketable and increasingly exportable product as well.

The potential uses for distillers grain are just beginning to be explored. Recently, plants have begun to experiment with a new and valuable product by passing distillers grain through a process using chemicals and high-pressure steam. The result? Plastic. Yes, plastic, the polymer present in just about every modern product.

And that's not all! About five percent of the material generated by the ethanol fermentation process is commercial corn oil. That's about 1.5 pounds of commercial corn oil per bushel of corn.[20] Corn oil has many uses, including as an additive to soap, paint, insecticides, textiles, inks, nitroglycerin, rustproofing, and pharmaceuticals.

Cellulosic Ethanol

Thanks to the miracles of science, there are ways to produce ethanol other than the fermentation of corn or sugarcane. Scientists are now working hard to produce more cellulosic ethanol, which, as I mentioned earlier, can be made from plant waste including corn cobs and stalks, grasses, wood, and many other plant materials. The only raw material needed to produce this kind of ethanol is cellulose, which forms the cell wall that makes a plant able to stand up.*****

Cellulosic ethanol realizes an advantage over ethanol from corn or

---

***** There are other experimental ways of producing small amounts of ethanol from something other than cellulose, but for the sake of simplicity, I've decided to lump all advanced ways of producing ethanol under the term "cellulosic ethanol."

sugarcane because it can be derived from virtually no-cost plant waste. It realizes a disadvantage, however, in that it currently costs much more per gallon to produce cellulosic ethanol than to produce corn ethanol because the process of breaking down the cellulose is much more expensive than fermenting the starch in corn.

Due to the current cost and difficulty of making it, projections suggest that actual output of cellulosic ethanol will fall short of government-projected output over the next several years.[21]

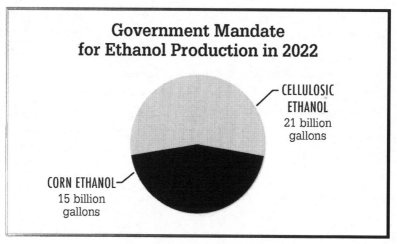

Government Mandate for Ethanol Production in 2022

CELLULOSIC ETHANOL
21 billion gallons

CORN ETHANOL
15 billion gallons

Source: Renewable Fuels Standard: Overview and Issues

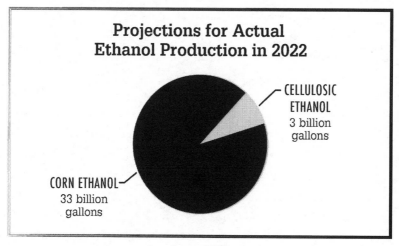

Projections for Actual Ethanol Production in 2022

CELLULOSIC ETHANOL
3 billion gallons

CORN ETHANOL
33 billion gallons

Source: POET

As you can see in the first graph, the original government mandate calls for 36 billion gallons of ethanol to be produced annually by 2022.[22] Of those 36 billion gallons, 15 billion are supposed to come from corn and 21 billion from cellulosic. At the time of this writing, it appears that cellulosic ethanol will not meet its 21-billion-gallon mandate in that time frame, but there is plenty of hope to suggest that advances in technology will improve the outlook.

Some companies have recently made great technological strides. One is Poet, Inc. Headquartered in South Dakota, Poet is the largest producer of ethanol in the world. In addition to producing 1.6 billion gallons of corn ethanol yearly, the company has constructed a new 25-million-gallon plant that uses corn stalks and other waste parts of the corn plant to produce cellulosic ethanol. Poet is also planning to add cellulosic production technology to each of their 26 corn ethanol production plants.

Meanwhile, DuPont, a multibillion-dollar corporation, has been working on cellulosic ethanol for ten years. They are currently constructing a 30-million-gallon-per-year plant. Six other companies are constructing plants for commercial production from five million gallons per year to 40 million gallons per year.

DuPont is also teaming up with another multibillion-dollar oil company, BP, to produce isobutanol, a product similar to ethanol but with some superior characteristics. A few ethanol production plants are experimenting with changes so they can produce isobutanol as well.

It would be a dream come true if cellulosic ethanol were to reach a high level of production. If this happened, Team Ethanol would be an even stronger competitor.

Conclusion

When compared to gasoline, both corn and cellulosic ethanol simply make better political, economic, and environmental sense. As gasoline becomes more expensive, the economic advantages of ethanol will increase substantially, eliminating any need for a mandate, subsidy, or government support of any kind. The production and distribution system for ethanol are in place already and getting better all the time. Producers and distributors are committing considerable effort to make E15 and E85 more available to consumers. Ethanol is a high-performance fuel, despite what you may have heard. It is a highly exportable commodity, and as demand increases, it will make a tremendous contribution to the US economy. Further, the byproducts of corn-based ethanol (distillers grain, corn oil, and possibly plastics) are valuable products.

All of this adds up to one clear picture: Once peak oil is reached and the price of gasoline becomes too high for the average consumer, the world is going to need all the ethanol it can possibly get. This makes Team Ethanol the strongest competitor in the Fuel Conference and a truly formidable opponent in the Clean Energy Bowl.

Ethanol: Myths and Truths

I n this chapter, I'll put to rest a number of misconceptions about ethanol—myths that have given the naysayers false fodder for years. If you ever find yourself in a discussion about these so-called flaws of ethanol in production or as a product, don't believe the hype (or the myth, as it were). In the following pages, I'll outline nine common myths about Team Ethanol and then dispel them with corresponding truths.

Myth #1: Ethanol creates less energy than is required to produce it.

The misperception here is that it takes so much effort and energy to produce a gallon of ethanol, you actually wind up costing yourself more energy than you produce. The argument is like saying it takes twice the effort to produce half the results. Well, in this case, the naysayers seem to have their facts exactly backward.

Truth: People seem to be confusing ethanol with gasoline.

It is true that, before 2003 when computerized ethanol-production plants were first built, the input energy to produce ethanol was more than the energy content of the ethanol. But because these new plants are computerized and production technology is so much more efficient, those figures have improved considerably. According to an analysis released by the US Department of Agriculture in June 2010, it takes only one unit of energy to create 2.3 units of ethanol energy.[1] So that's a net gain of 1.3 units of energy.

Maybe the people who believe this myth are actually confusing ethanol with gasoline. Researchers recently revealed that you need

1.23 units of fossil fuel to create one unit of energy in gasoline. That's a *loss* of 0.23 units of energy.

So let's get the facts straight: it's actually gasoline for which you have to put more energy into making it than you get out of it. All that gasoline we're currently using is actually *costing* us energy. Ethanol, contrary to what you might have heard, corrects that problem and then some.

Myth #2: Ethanol production is bad for the environment.

There are many angles to this argument. First, there's the misconception that ethanol plants produce enough greenhouse gas to render their product's greenhouse-gas-emission advantage irrelevant, with no total reduction in greenhouse gases. "Sure," the argument goes, "ethanol burns cleaner than gasoline, but those ethanol plants pump out too much greenhouse gas for that to matter."

Next, there's the idea that ethanol spills can be every bit as devastating to the soil and water as oil spills.

Third, some suggest that increasing ethanol production would lead to the need to increase total land required for corn or sugarcane, which would in turn lead to further destruction of the rainforest in Brazil.

Fourth, there's the argument that ethanol production requires too much water to be sustainable.

And finally, so they assert, ethanol plants produce too much physical waste.

Let's address these unfounded claims one by one.

Truth: Ethanol production and use substantially reduces net greenhouse gas emissions.

Independent studies have shown that ethanol, when considering exhaust as well as production emissions, reduces harmful greenhouse gases by up to as much as 59% compared to gasoline.[2] According to a US research laboratory, ethanol use reduces greenhouse gas emissions by 21.9 million tons.[3] That's like removing 3.5 million cars from the road.

Part of the reason for this is that ethanol contains so much oxygen (35%, according to studies).[4] With more oxygen in the fuel, more complete combustion occurs, and more complete combustion equals less pollution from the tailpipe.

The bottom-line truth is that gasoline is far worse for the environment than ethanol. Gasoline exhaust contains benzene, a cancer-causing agent, while in comparison, ethanol contains no benzene. So ethanol burns better and is less toxic.[5]

Truth: Ethanol spills do not harm the soil or water.

Studies have repeatedly concluded that ethanol poses very little threat to surface water or groundwater. Ethanol is alcohol in its purest form. Just alcohol. So when you spill it on the ground, it evaporates (and quite quickly at that). When you spill it in the water, ethanol quickly and naturally degrades. Compare this to an oil or gasoline spill. Spill oil or gas on land or water and the effects can be devastating to the wildlife that lives there.

Truth: Ethanol production will not lead to deforestation in the Amazon Rainforest

At present, Brazil is the second-largest producer of ethanol in the world, at eight billion gallons per year. Brazil also happens to be a country with huge amounts of rainforest land. The country currently meets all of its ethanol needs without encroaching on any rainforest land. In fact, all Brazil's sugarcane is produced in the south, 1,500 miles from the nearest rainforest. And that's not going to change, even with an increase in demand for the product. You can't grow sugarcane on or near rainforest land because you can't harvest sugarcane in lands as rainy year round as the rainforest. For one thing, sugarcane won't get ripe for harvest without a long enough period of dry weather. For another, sugarcane harvesting equipment just can't operate on such wet and muddy ground.

Further, Brazil boasts an immense amount of tillable land not currently used for agriculture. The six billion gallons of ethanol produced in Brazil come from only 1.4% of land on which sugarcane can be grown. Let's round that percentage up to 2%. So if Brazil can grow six billion gallons of ethanol on only 2% of the non-rainforest land currently available to use, then it's easy to see that more land should equate to much more ethanol. By my calculation, Brazil could produce as much as 150 billion gallons of ethanol without ever encroaching on the rainforest.

So that's 150 billion gallons out of the 180 billion we'll need by 2040 already in the bag, and that's just from Brazil. The US alone could produce the additional 30 billion gallons needed, and they could do that by doubling the current corn crop (and as I mentioned, that already appears possible, even likely).

Of course these numbers on their own are just theoretical, but they also ignore contributions from the rest of the world. If Brazil can't produce 150 billion gallons on its own, and the US can't produce 30 billion gallons on its own, there are plenty of other countries that could chip in. Out of the 111 countries currently growing corn, there are approximately 15 that could make a significant contribution to the world supply. The same is true for 15 of the 100 countries that currently grow sugarcane. Many of these countries are already increasing their corn and sugarcane production. Given technological advancements and currently available land, we have plenty of acreage in the world to more than meet present and future ethanol demands without encroaching on the rainforest.

Truth: The water use of an ethanol plant is very low, well managed, and recyclable, and it's getting better all the time.

First, let's get an important point out of the way: ethanol production doesn't require drinking water. The only water needed to produce ethanol can easily be gathered from the clean-water output of municipal waste plants.

Second, if you didn't see my footnote from the previous chapter about ethanol production, then I'm pleased to inform you that every ounce of the water used in the ethanol-making process is consumed or recycled in some form or another. The water that doesn't directly become ethanol winds up either as moisture in distillers grain, as clean steam released into the atmosphere, or in a drainage pool that allows the water to slowly and naturally evaporate. What this means is that, whether we're talking about air quality or water use, an ethanol plant is absolutely not damaging to the environment.

Third, if you think an ethanol plant uses too much water, then maybe you should shift your concern to America's many, many golf courses. In a full year, an ethanol plant uses only as much water as three golf courses. There are over 15,500 golf courses in the United States.[6] If you do the math (and if you'll forgive the pun), the water used by ethanol plants is only a drop in the bucket by comparison.

Truth: Ethanol production creates no waste.

At an ethanol production plant, the only inputs to the front end of the process are corn and water. On the back end, as I have mentioned, the output is ethanol, distillers grain, corn oil, steam, and some water—and nothing else. There is no waste of any kind from an ethanol plant.

Myth #3: The existing infrastructure cannot support an increase in ethanol use.

The idea here is that we've got this sprawling infrastructure of tankers, pipelines, and gas stations that are currently set up to transport and dispense only gasoline. Naysayers suggest it would cost a fortune to replace all those implements with ones designed to dispense ethanol. An interesting angle. Let's check its validity.

Truth: The cost of making slight changes to gasoline stations will be minimal compared to the projected economic success of the industry.

It is true that gas stations will require blender pumps and an underground storage tank to hold only ethanol. But according to some experts, providing America's gas stations with brand-new blender pumps and a storage tank devoted exclusively to holding ethanol would require a mere $10,000 per station. The station would recoup this investment easily because it now would have the advantage of selling many different blends of ethanol and gasoline.[7]

Myth #4: Cars don't perform as well on ethanol as they do on gasoline.

"You'll get lower gas mileage!" "You'll lose horsepower!" "Ethanol is for sissies!" None of this is true.

Truth: Engines can actually perform *better* with ethanol.

While it is technically true that you may lose about 30% of your mileage efficiency if you switch your older-model car to ethanol, it is also true that the latest-model engines are narrowing the gap significantly. Engines built to take advantage of the benefits of ethanol have reduced the deficit by a third. The disadvantage will continue shrinking as new technology is introduced and engines become more optimized to ethanol as a fuel source.[8]

As to the question of performance, you know the numbers you see on the front of the gas pump when you fuel up your car? They're numbers like 87 and 93. Those numbers refer to what's called an *octane rating*. The higher the octane, the more power delivered to the engine. An 87 refers to the octane rating of regular unleaded gasoline. A 93 refers to premium unleaded. Ethanol's octane rating? A whopping 113! This means more power and faster acceleration. That's why the gas tanks of Indy 500 and NASCAR drivers are no strangers to the product.

Myth #5: Ethanol will harm your car's engine.

I have no idea where the rumor came from, but it goes something like this: Your car was designed to use gasoline; if you put something other than gasoline into your tank, your motor will degrade faster than you can say "engine gunk." Ethanol opponents warn that your engine will run hotter. Also, don't you dare try to use it in cold weather, because ethanol will lead to your gas lines freezing. I'm going to try to put this lightly: every last one of these claims is ridiculous.

Truth: Ethanol keeps your engine *cleaner* than gasoline.

There is a simple reason why ethanol is clean: ethanol is alcohol. Pure, 100% alcohol. So what do we use alcohol for? In addition to drinking alcohol, in the form of vodka, for example, we use it for quite a few things, actually. Chief among them are sterilization and cleaning. Does that sound like it would lead to dirtier engine parts? Of course not.

Unlike gasoline, which leaves gummy deposits in your fuel line and your engine, ethanol burns completely, leaving no residue. Not only that, ethanol actually *cleans out* existing deposits. Studies have repeatedly shown that using ethanol reduces buildup in fuel injectors, filters, and lines.[9] It's like giving your fuel line and engine a cleansing bath.

Still, sometimes mechanics will tell you that it's the ethanol that's to blame for clogging up the fuel line. That could actually be *because* of ethanol's cleansing properties. It seems that when you first start using ethanol after having used gasoline for any appreciable amount of time, the ethanol cleans all the gasoline crud out of your fuel lines and pushes it into the carburetor and engine. This crud then needs to be cleaned out. So it isn't ethanol that's to blame; it's the fuel you were putting into your car before you started using ethanol.

Truth: Ethanol keeps your engine *cooler* than gasoline.

Again, ethanol is pure alcohol, and alcohol has many, many advantages over gasoline. Here we find another. Alcohol combusts at a lower temperature than does gasoline. The cooler-burning fuel tends to prevent wear and tear on engine valves. This is another part of the reason the fuel is so popular among Indy and NASCAR drivers. High horsepower leads to tremendous heat. Less heat means fewer problems while you're roaring around the track at 220mph.

Truth: Ethanol is like antifreeze for your gas line.

Here's another point where the myth is the complete opposite of the truth. When you run your engine on gasoline, you often have to buy additives like de-icers to prevent your fuel system from freezing up in the winter. That's not the case if you run your car on ethanol. Again, alcohol has many advantages. Among them, it simply does not freeze. Don't believe me? Try putting a bottle of rubbing alcohol in the freezer. Check back in a week and see what you see. Here's a hint: it will still be as liquid as it was the day you put it in there.

Myth #6: The more ethanol we produce, the less food we'll have.

This myth is commonly referred to as the "food versus fuel" debate. The idea is that if we need more ethanol to power our cars, then we'll need more corn to produce that ethanol. The more corn we dedicate to fuel, the less corn we'll have to eat and to feed our livestock. This phenomenon then drives up the cost of food overall.

Truth: Corn supply, demand, and price are not set in a vacuum.

The trouble with the claim that using corn for ethanol increases food prices is that it assumes corn production operates in a vacuum—as if we can only meet the added demand with *existing* corn crops, and cannot for any reason grow *more* corn. It also assumes that if we didn't use any corn for ethanol, farmers would grow the same amount of corn. Well, that's silly.

Truth: Allocating corn to ethanol production does not reduce the food and feed supply.

The primary reason the world's farmers do not grow more corn is that not enough people are willing to pay the farmers enough to grow it. It's simple economics.

I know I've made this point already, but let's look at the food versus fuel numbers one more time. The US currently grows about 13 billion bushels of corn per year. Out of that number, about 5.2 billion bushels goes into the ethanol production process. So that's approximately 40% of the current corn supply that goes to ethanol. You might assume that this leaves only 60% for livestock feed, but that would be incorrect. Remember, we still have distillers grain, which means that a full 1.6 billion of those original 5.2 billion bushels gets redistributed as livestock feed. So now we're only talking about 3.6 billion bushels of corn that ethanol takes away from the food supply, a mere 28%.

These numbers also ignore those economic principles I highlighted in the first paragraph. If the demand for corn is higher than the supply, whether for ethanol or for livestock feed, then the price for corn goes up, which in turn compels more farmers to plant more corn, which in turn meets the supply need. Bottom line: the production of ethanol does not lower the amount of corn available for food and livestock feed.

Myth #7: We don't have enough land to meet the demand for ethanol and food at the same time.

This argument runs as follows: The United States has already allocated all its land to residential areas, national parks, industrial grounds, commercial zones, and farmland. There just isn't any land left to expand into new corn fields. We have therefore maximized the total amount of corn we can hope to produce on our land.

This simply isn't so.

Truth: We've got all kinds of land to grow more food.

Let's ignore the farmland we're not using for crops at present and focus only on what we *are* using. Of the 434 million acres of farmland in the United States, we're currently using 72.1 million acres to grow corn. Even if we decide for some reason that we can't (or don't want to) expand the amount of land in production, the miracles of modern seed science will take care of the expansion for us. Continuous improvement in agricultural science has taken the number of bushels of corn capable of being grown on one acre of farmland from an average of 40 bushels per acre in the 1940s to an average of 173 per acre in the 2014 harvest.[10]

As previously mentioned, the developers of corn seed have indicated that they will be able to produce a seed that can yield 300 bushels per acre under average growing conditions, and even more under excellent growing conditions. Also, drought-resistant corn is being developed so that dry years will cause less damage to the corn crop.[11]

We have more land we could be using to grow food crops, and someday soon, all the land we already use will be producing much more corn than it produces currently. Then corn production will set new and much higher records.

Myth #8: The more ethanol we produce, the more expensive food will become.

This is the final line on the "food versus fuel" debate. It's based on the faulty assumption that the more ethanol we produce, the less food we'll have to feed our livestock. This assumption takes things one step further, claiming that if we have less food to feed our livestock, in turn causing feed prices to go up, then the rise in feed cost will be passed on to the consumer. The more ethanol we put into our cars, the more we'll pay for a hamburger.

Truth: Ethanol has very little to do with any increase in food prices.

There are many contributing factors here, but the one to focus on is that a number of new, independent studies have shown that food price spikes cannot be attributed to ethanol production.[12] I hate to belabor the point, but because of the distillers grain byproduct, ethanol does not take as much corn out of the food chain as is generally believed. Additionally, if the demand for corn rises, there is more than enough land worldwide to increase supply to where the prices would be more palatable. Corn is a globally traded commodity, after all, and despite what most people think, we have generally seen grain surpluses worldwide over the past 50 years.

Producing enough food for everyone worldwide is not a problem. Globally, we're using less than a third of the land available for crops like wheat, corn, or soybeans. The only reason we're not using more is because there aren't enough people willing to pay enough money for farmers to turn a profit by farming these available lands. Ethanol isn't the problem. It's straight economics.

Myth #9: Ethanol production is too expensive to be competitive.

The myth is that Team Ethanol is at a competitive disadvantage compared to Team Gasoline because it costs so much more to produce ethanol. As I mentioned in my introduction, that just isn't the case anymore.

Truth: Ethanol is generally cheaper to produce than gasoline.

In the 1980s, with old technology, ethanol was more expensive to produce. That situation lingers on in the minds of many people. Ethanol needed government subsidies to bring the price down to a moderate level.

However, the development of new processing technology and the computerization of ethanol production plants have caused two important things to happen. First, ethanol production plants no longer receive direct government subsidies (although there are still indirect subsidies).[13] Second, new production technology makes ethanol generally cheaper than gasoline.

All of these truths add up to my firm belief that Team Ethanol will be the long-term winner of the Fuel Conference. This sets this strong team up for a battle of the century against Team Nuclear. It is sure to be a compelling Clean Energy Bowl indeed. But before we watch it play out on the field, let's take one last look at Team Ethanol's greatest strengths.

Nine Reasons Ethanol Will Win the Fuel Conference

Now that we have crunched the numbers and examined the trends, let's look at a quick summary of the reasons I believe Team Ethanol will be the winner of the Fuel Conference and a strong competitor in the Clean Energy Bowl. As you might have noticed, my research concludes that there are many compelling reasons why Team Ethanol will win the Fuel Conference, but for the sake of offering a palatable primer of Team Ethanol's strengths, I have reduced the list to ten.

1. At least 90% of the world's cars will continue to use the internal combustion engine.

The ICE will remain dominant in the decades to come, thanks to two main factors. First is the staggering cost of the batteries needed to run hybrid and electric cars. Second, the ICE will eventually propel certain cars to 60 and perhaps even more mpg, all the while costing substantially less than hybrids, plug-in hybrids, or electric cars. With the rare and expensive metals and materials used in modern batteries likely to increase in cost, it stands to reason that the cost per battery won't be coming down anytime soon.[1] The competitively affordable hybrid or electric engine is a mirage.

2. Only two fuels work in the internal combustion engine.

The only practical fuels that work in the ICE are petroleum derivatives and ethanol. We have projected that ICEs will continue to propel at least 90% of the world's cars through 2030. We also know that projections suggest the total number of cars on the road worldwide will increase from one billion to two billion by that same year.

Meanwhile, when the shale oil bubble bursts, and as the decline of conventional oil wells continues worldwide, this will lead directly to a global demand for 180 billion gallons of ethanol per year by 2040.

3. Once global oil peaks, the economic strength of ethanol will far outpace that of any other method of producing fuel for ICEs.

Peak oil makes for a bleak picture for Team Gasoline. That picture is only going to get bleaker every year as gasoline production falls shorter and shorter of demand. Ethanol will be the only practical competitor available to make up that shortfall. This will leave Team Ethanol with a competitive advantage, given that it can price itself at a point below that of gasoline.

4. Ethanol is the only way to become truly fuel independent.

Way back in the first chapter, I highlighted the point that, when politicians say "energy independent," what they really mean is "fuel independent." The United States is already electricity independent. The only energy resource we import comes on the fuel side.

The United States holds 4% of the world's petroleum reserves (including recoverable shale oil and oil shale) while OPEC holds 73%. More drilling here at home isn't the long-term answer. The only way to move toward long-term fuel independence and reduce the cost of fuel is to make and use more ethanol here at home. It makes sense to begin to build and support the infrastructure to produce and distribute ethanol, so as not to be caught flatfooted when the oil price begins to soar.

5. The world can produce a sufficient amount of corn and sugarcane to meet ethanol demand at a reasonable market price.

There are three main reasons that corn and sugarcane yields per acre will increase. The first is genetic science applied to seeds. With seed technology improving all the time, the world will reach a 300 bushel per acre yield and increase the yield for sugarcane as well.

The second is improvement in a broad range of corn and sugarcane planting and harvesting technologies, including no-till planting, insect and disease control, water management, soil preservation, and more efficient harvesting.

The third is sufficient available land. There's enough land for the world to grow enough corn and sugarcane to easily produce 180 billion gallons of ethanol without using any land from the rainforest or other ecologically sensitive areas. Economically speaking, since the demand for ethanol will create a reward opportunity for corn and sugarcane growers, there will be plenty of incentive to produce enough of these two renewable commodities to meet demand.

6. Eventually ethanol will no longer need government mandates or supportive policies.

Two main factors are at work here. Research shows that ethanol typically costs about 50 cents per gallon less than gasoline. At that price, sellers of gasoline can blend ethanol into their gasoline and make more money. Let's say they buy ethanol for $2.50 per gallon and sell it for $3.00 per gallon mixed into gasoline. Even if the cost of transportation and blending cuts gasoline company profit to 20 cents per gallon, it results in a free-market incentive for gasoline companies to buy ethanol.

The second factor is the often-stated coming of peak oil precipitating increased gasoline prices and increased demand for ethanol. As demand increases from the free market need for ethanol, government support (whether as mandates or otherwise) will no longer be necessary.

7. When the price of oil soars, it is highly unlikely that there will ever be the kind of ethanol surplus necessary to drive the price of ethanol down.

There's a number of contributing factors to this statement, but the chief factor is that demand for ethanol will increase enormously after peak oil is reached. Gasoline prices will start their upward climb while ethanol sells at a price well below that of gasoline.

Another factor is that, with developing countries buying a rapidly increasing number of cars, the upward slope of demand for ethanol will rival that of the steepest mountain.

In addition, export channels are opening up, which will only make it easier to deliver the supply from ethanol-producing countries to countries demanding more ethanol. Some developed nations of the world—particularly in Europe, Japan, and other parts of Asia—have very little land on which to grow corn and sugarcane. These areas will need to meet their fuel requirements with an enormous amount of imported ethanol.

Considering these factors, it will be difficult for ethanol producers to construct new plants and create new ethanol quickly enough to keep up with such a sharp increase in demand. It will be so difficult, in fact, that it almost seems foolhardy to suggest an oversupply of ethanol.

8. Ethanol is better for the environment than gasoline, both in terms of particulate matter and human-caused global warming.

Here it is in black and white: Gasoline is far more polluting than ethanol. One way to make a significant reduction in CO_2 emissions is to change the fuel we use from gasoline to ethanol. A full switch to ethanol could reduce harmful greenhouse gas emissions by up to 59%.[2] Making this switch would also eliminate the carcinogenic benzene that gasoline exhaust emits into the air we breathe. If you want to make a difference in the environment, ethanol over gasoline is the logical way to go.

9. The US national interest resides in the increased use of ethanol.

It has long been the stated goal of US politicians to unshackle the United States from its dependence on foreign oil. This would create domestic economic growth, more jobs, and better national security. But if we're talking about making the United States permanently independent of foreign oil by using only domestic oil, what we're actually talking about is a fairy tale—at least for as long as OPEC nations control 73% of world oil reserves to the mere 4% held by the US.

Talking about the United States working toward fuel independence without the use of ethanol is about the same as telling your children that the Easter Bunny and the Tooth Fairy really exist. As parents, we know it's not true, and yet our children still tend to believe the stories for years. Well, in this analogy, politicians are the parents and the unwitting public is the children. For years, we've been led to believe that the global oil outlook is better than it is, and that domestic oil production potential (thanks to shale oil and oil shale) will save us from our insatiable demand, most of which will eventually be filled by foreign oil.

Unfortunately, as long as the media continues to pay so little attention to the approaching oil and fuel crisis, too many Americans will continue to believe in the Tooth Fairy that is fuel independence without ethanol.

US Fuel independence is possible—and I posit that it is *only* possible—if the country works toward building additional infrastructure to allow for increased production and use of ethanol. Between its capacity to grow exponentially more corn and with many places in the South where sugarcane could be grown to supplement that high capacity, the United States could continue to be the world leader in ethanol production, solving the coming fuel crisis while simultaneously benefiting economic growth here at home.

With all these advantages over the other competitors, I am confident that Team Ethanol will be the runaway victor of the Fuel Conference. The only question remaining is this: of our two champions, Team Ethanol and Team Nuclear, who will win the Clean Energy Bowl?

CONCLUSION

Who Will Win the Clean Energy Bowl?

When I first set out to write this book, I was quite confident that, after I had completed my research, I would be able to project the winner of the Clean Energy Bowl with ease. I am still confident, but I must admit that the more research I conducted, the more hesitant I was to designate an outright champion. While neither team playing in the Clean Energy Bowl is the star of its conference at the time of this writing (Team Coal and Team Gasoline still rule), both Team Nuclear and Team Ethanol present compelling cases to win the big game. The ultimate winner, however, will be the team that demonstrates the greatest positive impact on the world economy while reducing particulate pollution and the emission of greenhouse gases over the next 20 years and beyond. In other words, the winner will be the one team that most improves the standard of living worldwide over the long term.

Both teams are currently winners when it comes to the production and use of their products. Corn and sugarcane ethanol production is massive and cost effective; nuclear-produced electricity is expanding across the globe. Both Team Ethanol and Team Nuclear are working on new technologies that have the potential to transform the world into a better place. The breakthrough technology for Team Nuclear is the widespread production and use of Small Modular Reactors (SMRs), with Traveling Wave Reactors (TWRs) as an equally exciting technology not far behind. With that in mind, if we want to make the best prediction about who will win the Clean Energy Bowl, we have to answer this question: Which breakthrough technology is most likely to be successful and make a greater contribution to raising the standard of living in the world?

On the one hand, Team Ethanol can enhance the transportation sector of the economy by providing reasonably priced fuel, but its success in doing so depends primarily on whether oil prices increase fast enough for ethanol to become a commanding player in supplying fuel for all those ICEs. If it can find a way to produce huge amounts of cost-effective cellulosic ethanol, then it will absolutely change the game. Not only would such an advance virtually eliminate opposition to increased ethanol production (the "food versus fuel" debate would be even more moot); it would also enhance Team Ethanol's claim to being a low-emissions replacement for gasoline. At the moment, however, the process required to convert plant waste into ethanol has proven too difficult and costly. That certainly could change, but at present I'm not ready to call cellulosic ethanol a viable technological advantage.

As for Team Nuclear, the strength of its team depends on its prospects for assuring the public that it is a safe provider of electricity, can be economically feasible on a consistent basis, can find safe and effective methods for storing and recycling waste, and can do all this while boasting no particulate pollution or greenhouse gas emissions. To be declared the winner of the Clean Energy Bowl, Team Nuclear must demonstrate its potential to make massive progress with its public-relations situation before it can hope to provide billions of people with sufficient electricity.

I believe that the history of small nuclear reactors in submarines (and in approximately 130 other places in the world) gives every indication that the new SMR technology, including mass factory-line production, will work and become widespread. There are many countries currently planning to mass-produce SMRs and export them around the world. With monetary and technological support from developed countries to make SMRs available to developing countries, there will be few if any technological barriers to providing electricity to many if not most of the approximately 3 billion people in the world who have access to insufficient or even no electricity.[1]

I believe that SMRs demonstrate a greater chance of contributing to Team Nuclear's goals than cellulosic ethanol has for contributing to Team Ethanol's goals.

So now, without further ado, I offer my prediction as to the winner of the Clean Energy Bowl. Drum roll please...

The team that will do the most to raise the standard of living in the world by simultaneously providing an efficient and effective source of energy while also producing little to no particulate pollution or greenhouse gases is Team Nuclear.

While both teams make sense in their ability to improve and build upon the world economy, and while both can lay claim to helping the environment, it is ultimately Team Nuclear's potential to change *nearly everything* for at least three billion people who have little or no electricity that tips the scale in its favor. Team Ethanol can and will help billions of new people drive cars in the coming decades, but Team Nuclear will literally create a new and better life for over 40% of the world's population while also adding massive amounts of safe and efficient electricity to already-developed countries. And it will do all of this while producing *zero* greenhouse gas emissions.

No matter what the future brings, it appears clear that both Team Ethanol and Team Nuclear stand the best chance of boosting the American economy while simultaneously stemming the tide of global warming. While Team Nuclear is the winner of the Clean Energy Bowl, embracing both teams will revolutionize the way we think about energy in this country. With cheaper, lower-emission, and completely renewable fuel from ethanol, and with cheap, totally clean, and absolutely safe electricity from nuclear power, we *all* win.

About the Author

Gary Schwendiman graduated with honors from Washington State University and earned his Master of Science and PhD degrees from Brigham Young University. He is cofounder of a private equity firm that invests in clean energy and has given presentations on clean energy in 26 states and 10 foreign countries.

He was a professor at the General Motors Institute. He served for 17 years as the Dean of the College of Business Administration at the University of Nebraska. As dean, he provided academic leadership for 70 PhD faculty members, 3,000 undergraduate students, and 150 graduate students. He has served on the boards of directors of five corporations.

He is the father of five children and grandfather of 14. He lives in Tucson, Arizona.

Endnotes

Introduction

[1] Bianca Mulaney, "Meeting Warren Buffett," *The Harvard Independent*, April 12, 2014, http://www.harvardindependent.com/2014/04/meeting-warren-buffett/.

Chapter 1

[1] NASA, "What's in a Name? Global Warming vs. Climate Change," NASA, "Weather and Climate," accessed July 1, 2015, http://pmm.nasa.gov/education/articles/whats-name-global-warming-vs-climate-change.

[2] Rachelle Oblack, "Global Warming vs. Climate Change," *About Education*, accessed December 4, 2014, http://weather.about.com/od/climatechange/f/global_warming_climate_change.htm.

Philip Ross, "Cow Farts Have 'Larger Greenhouse Gas Impact' Than Previously Thought; Methane Pushes Climate Change," *International Business Times*, November 26, 2013, http://www.ibtimes.com/cow-farts-have-larger-greenhouse-gas-impact-previously-thought-methane-pushes-climate-change-1487502.

[3] Jeffrey Lee, "Milankovitch Cycles," in *The Encyclopedia of Earth 2012*, National Council for Science and the Environment and Boston University, http://www.eoearth.org/view/article/154612/.

"The Astronomical Theory of the Ice Age" infographic, Rice Space Institute, October 7, 2002, http://earth.rice.edu/mtpe/cryo/cryosphere/topics/ice_age/compare.html.

Robert Kunzig, "Climate Milestone: Earth's CO_2 Level Passes 400ppm," *National Geographic*, May 9, 2013, http://news.nationalgeographic.com/news/energy/2013/05/130510-earth-co2-milestone-400-ppm/.

[4] John Cook, What the science says..." *Skeptical Science,* accessed December 15, 2014, http://www.skepticalscience.com/venus-runaway-greenhouse-effect.htm.

[5] Paula Aven Gladitch, "Only 72 Percent of Americans Saving for Retirement," Benefitspro.com, March 17, 2014, http://www.benefitspro.com/2014/03/17/only-72-percent-of-americans-saving-for-retirement.

[6] Lyndon Johnson, private comment, quoted in John Kenneth Galbraith, *Name-Dropping: From FDR On,* Wilmington, MA: Mariner Books, 1999, 149.

[7] "Coal," Institute for Energy Research, accessed May 22, 2014, http://www.instituteforenergyresearch.org/energy-overview/coal.

[8] Rudy Giuliani, Republican debate, January 24, 2008, http://www.ontheissues.org/Archive/2008_GOP_FL_Rudy_Giuliani.htm.

[9] US Energy Information Administration, "Technically Recoverable Shale Oil and Shale Gas Resources: An Assessment of 137 Shale Formations in 41 Countries Outside the US," corrected version, Washington, DC, US Department of Energy June, 2013, http://www.eia.gov/analysis/studies/worldshalegas/pdf/fullreport.pdf.

[10] Steve Fetter, "How Long Will the World's Uranium Supplies Last?" *Scientific American,* January 26, 2009, http://www.scientificamerican.com/article/how-long-will-global-uranium-deposits-last/.

[11] International Energy Agency, *World Energy Outlook 2012,* Paris, France, International Energy Agency, 90, http://www.iea.org/publications/freepublications/publication/WEO2012_free.pdf.

[12] Population Research Bureau, "World Population Data Sheet 2012: An Interactive Map," accessed August 15, 2014, http://www.prb.org/Publications/Datasheets/2012/world-population-data-sheet/world-map.aspx#/map/population.

[13] Frano Barbir, Sergio Ulgiati, *Sustainable Energy Production and Consumption: Benefits, Strategies and Environmental Costing,* Springer Science and Business Media, 2008, p.27.

[14] Conglin Xu, Laura Bell, "Global reserves, oil production show increase for 2014," December 1, 2014, accessed May 30, 2015, http://www.ogj.com/articles/print/volume-112/issue-12/special-report-worldwide-report/global-reserves-oil-production-show-increases-for-2014.html.

Chapter 2

[1] John Roberts, "Mini-nuclear plants the next frontier of US power supply – or the next Solyndra?"Executive, Fox News, July 30, 2013, accessed February 24, 2015, http://www.foxnews.com/politics/2013/07/30/mini-nuclear-plants-next-frontier-us-power-supply-or-next-solyndra/.

[2] Mark Clayton, "Nuclear Power: Obama Team Touts Mini-Nukes to Fight Global Warming," Christian Science Monitor, March 30, 2010, http://www.csmonitor.com/USA/2010/0330/Nuclear-power-Obama-team-touts-mini-nukes-to-fight-global-warming.

[3] Richard Schlesinger, "Nuclear Aims Small: The Real Nuclear Renaissance?" EnergyBiz Magazine, September/October 2012, http://www.energybiz.com/magazine/article/281595/nuclear-aims-small. For a comprehensive rundown of the different SMR designs, see the World Nuclear Association's "Small Nuclear Power Reactors," updated May 9, 2014, http://www.world-nuclear.org/info/Nuclear-Fuel-Cycle/Power-Reactors/Small-Nuclear-Power-Reactors/.

[4] US Energy Information Administration, "Levelized Cost of New Generation Resources in the Annual Energy Outlook 2011," Washington, DC: Energy Information Administration, December 2010, 3–4, http://www.eia.gov/oiaf/aeo/pdf/2016levelized_costs_aeo2011.pdf.

[5] "Processing of Used Nuclear Fuel," Information Library, World Nuclear Association, updated September 2014, accessed February 24, 2015, http://www.world-nuclear.org/info/nuclear-fuel-cycle/fuel-recycling/processing-of-used-nuclear-fuel/.

[6] "Coal Regains Some Electric Generation Market Share from Natural Gas," Today in Energy, May 23, 2013, http://www.eia.gov/todayinenergy/detail.cfm?id=11391.

[7] "World Nuclear Power Reactors and Uranium Requirements," World Nuclear Association, April 1, 2014, http://www.world-nuclear.org/info/Facts-and-Figures/World-Nuclear-Power-Reactors-and-Uranium-Requirements/.

[8] Antony Ingram, "Volkswagen Golf BlueMotion: 70 MPG Hatchback ... US Won't Get," Green Car Reports, March 5, 2014, http://www.greencarreports.com/news/1082723_volkswagen-golf-bluemotion-70-mpg-hatchback-u-s-wont-get.

Kirby Garlitos, "2013 Trident Iceni Grand Tourer," TopSpeed, August 23, 2012, http://www.topspeed.com/cars/others/2013-trident-iceni-grand-tourer-ar134041.html.

[9] "Gas Station Statistics," Statisticbrain.com, accessed January 1, 2014, http://statisticbrain.com/gas-station-statistics.

[10] Energy Information Administration, "Top World Oil Consumers, 2013," *EIA Frequently Asked Questions*, accessed February 26, 2015, http://www.eia.gov/countries/index.cfm?topL=con.

Dr. Edward Yardeni, *Energy Briefing: Crude Oil Demand and Supply*, Yardeni Research, February 24, 2015, http://paperzz.com/doc/3736883/energy-briefing--global-crude-oil-demand-%26-supply.

[11] Energy Information Administration, "When was the last refinery built in the United States?" Energy Information Administration, FAQ, updated July 1, 2015, accessed August 8, 2015, http://www.eia.gov/tools/faqs/faq.cfm?id=29&t=9.

[12] "Gasoline Stations with Convenience Stores (NAICS 44711)," US Census Bureau, last modified April 25, 2013, http://www.census.gov/econ/census/pdf/44711.pdf.

[13] Adam J. Liska, Haishun S. Yang, Virgil R. Bremer, Terry J. Klopfenstein, Daniel T. Walters, Galen E. Erickson, and Kevin G. Cassman, "Improvements in Life Cycle Energy Efficiency and Greenhouse Gas Emissions of Corn Ethanol," *Journal of Industrial Ecology*, 2008, DOI: 10.1111/j.1530-9290.2008.105x.

[14] American Cancer Society, "Benzene," *Learn About Cancer—Other Carcinogens, In the Workplace*, last revised December 9, 2013, accessed March 25, 2015, http://www.cancer.org/cancer/cancercauses/othercarcinogens/intheworkplace/benzene.

[15] Monsanto, "Our Commitment to Sustainable Agriculture," *Commitments*, Monsanto 2012, accessed December 25, 2014, http://sustainability.monsanto.com/commitments/our-commitment-to-sustainable-agriculture.

Chapter 3

[1] "World Nuclear Power Reactors," see note 4, Ch. 2, above.

[2] "Plans for New Reactors Worldwide," World Nuclear Association, updated March 2013, http://www.world-nuclear.org/info/Current-and-Future-Generation/Plans-For-New-Reactors-Worldwide/.

[3] "Achieving Universal Energy Access," United Nations Foundation, http://www.unfoundation.org/what-we-do/issues/energy-and-climate/clean-energy-development.html.

"Household Air Pollution and Health," World Health Organization, accessed September 26, 2014, http://www.who.int/mediacentre/factsheets/fs292/en/.

[4] "Nuclear Century Outlook," World Nuclear Association, published 2008, revised introduction 2012, accessed May 24, 2014, http://www.world-nuclear.org/WNA/Publications/WNA-Reports/WNA-Nuclear-Century-Outlook/.

[5] Ibid.

[6] Steve Hargreaves, "First New Nuclear Reactors OK'd in Over 30 Years," *CNN Money*, February 9, 2012, http://money.cnn.com/2012/02/09/news/economy/nuclear_reactors/.

[7] "The Nuclear Renaissance," World Nuclear Association, updated 2014, accessed May 24, 2014, http://world-nuclear.org/info/Current-and-Future-Generation/The-Nuclear-Renaissance/.

[8] The New York Times, *Guide to Essential Knowledge; Completely Revised and Expanded Edition*, New York, St. Martin's Press, 2011.

[9] New Jersey Department of Environmental Protection comments on draft EPA 111(d) rule, Nov. 26, 2014, quoted in Nuclear Energy Institute, "Fact Sheets, Nuclear Energy: America's Low-Carbon Electricity Leader," Backgrounders, November 2015, accessed January 12, 2016, http://www.nei.org/Master-Document-Folder/Backgrounders/Fact-Sheets/Nuclear-Energy-America-s-Low-Carbon-Electricity-Le.

[10] Bobby Magill, "Nuclear Power Needs to Double to Meet Warming Goal," Climate Central, January 29, 2015, accessed January 12, 2016, http://www.climatecentral.org/news/nuclear-power-needs-to-double-to-meet-warming-goal-18610 citing Nuclear Energy Agency, International Energy Agency, "Technology Roadmap, Nuclear Energy," 2015 edition, accessed January 12, 2016, http://www.iea.org/publications/freepublications/publication/TechnologyRoadmapNuclearEnergy.pdf.

[11] Nuclear Energy Institute, "Economic Growth and Job Creation," *Why Nuclear Energy?* Accessed January 12, 2016, http://www.nei.org/Why-Nuclear-Energy/Economic-Growth-Job-Creation.

[12] Frank von Hippel, Thomas B. Cochran, Harold A. Feiveson, Walt Patterson, Gennadi Pshakin, M.V. Ramana, Mycle Schneider, Tatsujiro Suzuki, *Fast Breeder Reactor Programs: History and Status*, Princeton, NJ: The International Panel on Fissile Materials, February 2010, http://fissilematerials.org/library/rr08.pdf.

Placid Rodriguez and S. M. Lee, "Who is Afraid of Breeders?" Indira Gandhi Centre for Atomic Research, November 1998, http://www.iisc.ernet.in/currsci/nov251998/articles13.htm.

[13] America Pink, "Fuel Efficiency and Types of Nuclear Waste," *Breeder Reactor*, accessed January 12, 2016, http://america.pink/breeder-reactor_744454.html.

[14] World Nuclear Association, "Nuclear-Powered Ships," Information Library, Transport, May 2015, accessed May 20, 2015, http://www.world-nuclear.org/info/non-power-nuclear-applications/transport/nuclear-powered-ships/.

[15] John Roberts, "Mini-nuclear plants the next frontier of US power supply – or the next Solyndra?"*Executive*, Fox News, July 30, 2013, accessed February 24, 2015, http://www.foxnews.com/politics/2013/07/30/mini-nuclear-plants-next-frontier-us-power-supply-or-next-solyndra/.

[16] Taxpayers for Common Sense, "Taxpayer Subsidies for Small Modular Reactors," February 27, 2013, updated September 30, 2015, accessed March 5, 2016, http://www.taxpayer.net/library/article/taxpayer-subsidies-for-small-modular-reactors.

[17] "Small and Medium Sized Reactors (SMRs) Development, Assessment, and Deployment," International Atomic Energy Agency, May 15, 2012, http://www.iaea.org/NuclearPower/SMR/.

"Small Modular Nuclear Reactors," see note 17, above.

[18] David Szondy, "Small Modular Nuclear Reactors—The Future of Energy?" *Gizmag.com*, February 16, 2012, http://www.gizmag.com/small-modular-nuclear-reactors/20860/.

[19] World Bank, "Agriculture and Rural Development," *Data*, The World Bank, accessed December 22, 2014, http://data.worldbank.org/topic/agriculture-and-rural-development.

[20] Paul Brown, "Is There a New Nuclear Kid on the Block?" *Scientific American*, January 8, 2014, http://www.scientificamerican.com/article/is-there-a-new-nuclear-kid-on-the-block/.

[21] "Small Nuclear Power Reactors," World Nuclear Association, May 9, 2013, http://www.world-nuclear.org/info/Nuclear-Fuel-Cycle/Power-Reactors/Small-Nuclear-Power-Reactors/.

[22] "Household Air Pollution and Health," World Health Organization, http://www.who.int/mediacentre/factsheets/fs292/en/.

[23] Matthew L. Wald, "The Next Nuclear Reactor May Arrive Hauled by a Truck," *New York Times*, April 24, 2013, http://www.nytimes.com/2013/04/25/business/energy-environment/the-next-nuclear-reactor-may-arrive-hauled-by-a-truck.html?pagewanted=all&_r=0.

[24] Stephen M. Goldberg and Robert Rosner, "Nuclear Reactors: Generation to Generation" (Cambridge, MA: American Academy of Arts and Sciences, 2011), http://www.amacad.org/multimedia/pdfs/publications/researchpapersmonographs/nuclearReactors.pdf.

[25] "Achieving Universal Energy Access," see note 3, above.

[26] "Household Air Pollution and Health," World Health Organization, accessed September 26, 2014, http://www.who.int/mediacentre/factsheets/fs292/en/.

[27] "Achieving Universal Energy Access," 66, see note 3, above.

[28] Kate Kunkel, "Small Nuclear Reactors—The Future of Nuclear?" NuScale Power, September 2011, http://www.nuscalepower.com/pdf/nuclear-exchange-sept-2011.pdf.

[29] Mark Clayton, "Nuclear Power: Obama Team Touts Mini-Nukes to Fight Global Warming," *Christian Science Monitor*, March 30, 2010, http://www.csmonitor.com/USA/2010/0330/Nuclear-power-Obama-team-touts-mini-nukes-to-fight-global-warming.

[30] Nuclear Matters, "The Day of Transportable, Refrigerator-Sized Nuclear Reactor Nears," *Homeland Security News Wire*, May 19, 2010, http://www.homelandsecuritynewswire.com/day-transportable-refrigerator-size-nuclear-reactor-nears.

[31] "Achieving Universal Energy Access," 67, see note 3, above.

[32] "US Nuclear Power Policy," World Nuclear Association, December 2014, http://www.world-nuclear.org/info/Country-Profiles/Countries-T-Z/USA--Nuclear-Power-Policy/.

Chapter 4

[1] Embassy of France in Washington, "Nuclear Energy in France," France in the United States, December 13, 2012, accessed December 30, 2014, http://ambafrance-us.org/spip.php?article949#.

[2] James Jukwey and Jane Baird, eds., "Update 1—France's power net exports fall in 2012—grid," *UK Reuters*, January 22, 2012, http://uk.reuters.com/article/2013/01/22/france-power-grid-idUKL6N0AR6EN20130122.

[3] Jon Palfreman, "Why the French like Nuclear Energy," *Readings, Frontline*, accessed December 14, 2014, http://www.pbs.org/wgbh/pages/frontline/shows/reaction/readings/french.html.

[4] Robert Bryce, "The Real Climate 'Deniers' Are the Greens," *Wall Street Journal*, February 2, 2012, http://online.wsj.com/news/articles/SB10001424052702304007504579346774109467020.

[5] Edward Goldsmith and Nicholas Hildyard, "Dams, failures and earthquakes," excerpted from The Social and Environmental Effects of Large Dams: Volume 1. Overview. Wadebridge Ecological Centre, Worthyvale Manor Camelford, Cornwall PL32 9TT. January 1, 1984, accessed August 11, 2015, http://www.edwardgoldsmith. org/1020/dams-failures-and-earthquakes/?show=all#.

"Dam Failures and Incidents," Association of State Dam Safety Officials, accessed August 11, 2015, http://www.damsafety.org/ news/?p=412f29c8-3fd8-4529-b5c9-8d47364c1f3e.

[6] World Nuclear Association, "Safety of Nuclear Power Reactors," World Nuclear Association Information Library, February 2015, accessed March 31, 2015, http://www.world-nuclear.org/info/safety-and-security/safety-of-plants/ safety-of-nuclear-power-reactors/.

[7] Brian Dunning, "Rethinking Nuclear Power," Skeptoid Media, March 18, 2008, http://skeptoid.com/episodes/4092.

[8] Ibid.

[9] Christian Nordqvist, "What is X-ray Exposure? How Safe Are Repeated X-rays?" Medical News Today, March 23, 2011, http://www.medicalnewstoday.com/ articles/219970.php.

[10] International Atomic Energy Agency, "Design of Reactor Containment Systems for Nuclear Power Plants: Safety Guide," Safety Standards Series, IAEA, Vienna, 2004, http://www-pub.iaea.org/MTCD/publications/PDF/Pub1189_web.pdf.

Joseph Gonyeau, P.E., "Key Areas and Buildings at the Nuclear Power Plant Site," The Virtual Nuclear Tourist, December 8, 2005, accessed March 9, 2015, http://www. nucleartourist.com/areas/areas.htm.

[11] Brian K. Grimes, "Information Notice No.93-53: Effect of Hurricane Andrew on Turkey Point Nuclear Generating Station and Lessons Learned," United States Nuclear Regulatory Commission, Office of Nuclear Reactor Regulation, Washington, DC, July 20, 1993, reviewed/ updated May 22, 2015, http://www.nrc.gov/reading-rm/ doc-collections/gen-comm/info-notices/1993/in93053.html.

[12] Markus Pössel, "From E=mc^2 to the Atomic Bomb," Einstein Online, vol. 04 (2010), 1004, http://www.einstein-online.info/spotlights/atombombe.

[13] Richard Rhodes, Nuclear Renewal: Common Sense about Energy, New York: Viking Press, 1993.

[14] World Nuclear Association, "Chernobyl Accident 1986," World Nuclear Association, updated April 2015, accessed August 24, 2015, http://www.world-nuclear.org/info/Safety-and-Security/Safety-of-Plants/Chernobyl-Accident/.

[15] Jayshree Suresh and B. S. Raghavan, *Human Values and Professional Ethics,* New Delhi: S. Chand and Company, 2009.

[16] Zhores A. Medvedev, *The Legacy of Chernobyl,* New York: W. W. Norton, 1993.

[17] "Chernobyl Accident 1986," World Nuclear Association, April 2014, http://www.world-nuclear.org/info/safety-and-security/safety-of-plants/chernobyl-accident/.

[18] Rhodes, "Nuclear Renewal," 79, see note 8, above.

[19] John Watson, "Japan's radiation disaster toll: none dead, none sick," *The Age,* June 4, 2013, accessed May 20, 2015, http://www.theage.com.au/comment/japans-radiation-disaster-toll-none-dead-none-sick-20130604-2nomz.html.

[20] Ibid.

[21] Robert Perkins, "Fukushima Disaster was Preventable, New Study Finds," USC News, September 21, 2015, accessed January 12, 2016, https://news.usc.edu/86362/fukushima-disaster-was-preventable-new-study-finds/.

[22] Wikipedia, "869 Sanriku Earthquake," Wikipedia, November 15, 2014, accessed December 15, 2014, http://en.wikipedia.org/wiki/869_Sanriku_earthquake.

Wikipedia, "1896 Sanriku Earthquake," Wikipedia, August 14, 2014, accessed December 15, 2014, http://en.wikipedia.org/wiki/1896_Sanriku_earthquake.

Wikipedia, "1933 Sanriku Earthquake," December 25, 2014, accessed December 29, 2014, http://en.wikipedia.org/wiki/1933_Sanriku_earthquake.

[23] "Japan: Fukushima Nuclear Disaster Caused by Arrogance," *Euronews,* July 23, 2012, http://www.euronews.com/2012/07/23/japan-fukushima-nuclear-disaster-caused-by-arrogance/.

[24] Ibid.

[25] "World Nuclear Power Reactors and Uranium Requirements," World Nuclear Association, April 1, 2014, http://www.world-nuclear.org/info/Facts-and-Figures/World-Nuclear-Power-Reactors-and-Uranium-Requirements/.

[26] "Supply of Uranium," World Nuclear Association, August 2012, http://www.world-nuclear.org/info/Nuclear-Fuel-Cycle/Uranium-Resources/Supply-of-Uranium/.

[27] James Hopf, "World Uranium Reserves," American Energy Independence, November 2004, http://www.americanenergyindependence.com/uranium.aspx.

[28] Ibid.

[29] Thor Energy, "Why Thorium?" *Thor Energy, Scandinavian Advanced Technology*, accessed January 12, 2016, http://thorenergy.no.s13.subsys.net/#thorium.

[30] Thor Energy, "Thorium as Nuclear Fuel," *Thor Energy, Scandinavian Advanced Technology*, accessed November 19, 2014, http://www.thorenergy.no/no/Topmenu/Thorium/Challenges-and-possibilities.aspx.

[31] The Weinberg Foundation Blog, "Posts Tagged Thorium"—a variety of news stories of thorium-adopters worldwide. Accessed November 19, 2014, http://www.the-weinberg-foundation.org/tag/thorium/.

[32] The Weinberg Foundation, "Thorium-Fuelled Molten Salt Reactors," Report for the All Party Parliamentary Group on Thorium Energy, The Weinberg Foundation, June 2013, p. 6. http://www.the-weinberg-foundation.org/wp-content/uploads/2013/06/Thorium-Fuelled-Molten-Salt-Reactors-Weinberg-Foundation.pdf.

[33] A. Nuttin, D. Heuer, A. Billebaud, R. Brissot, C. Le Brun, E. Liatard, J.-M. Loiseaux, L. Mathieu, O. Meplan, E. Merle-Lucotte, H. Nifenecker, F. Perdu, "Potential of Thorium Molten-Salt Reactors: Detailed Calculations and Concept Evolution with a View to Large Scale Energy Production," *Progress in Nuclear Energy*, Vol. 46, No. 1, pp. 77-99, 2005; doi: 10.1016/j.pnucene.2004.11.0011.

[34] Roger Harrabin, "Thorium backed as a 'future fuel'," BBC News, October 31, 2013, http://www.bbc.com/news/science-environment-24638816.

[35] Marin Katusa, "The Thing About Thorium: Why the Better Nuclear Fuel May Not Get a Chance," p. 3, Forbes.com, February 16, 2012, http://www.forbes.com/sites/energysource/2012/02/16/the-thing-about-thorium-why-the-better-nuclear-fuel-may-not-get-a-chance/3/.

What is Nuclear.com, "Thorium as Nuclear Fuel," What is Nuclear.com, accessed November 21, 2014, http://www.whatisnuclear.com/articles/thorium.html.

[36] "Thorium-Fuelled Molten Salt Reactors," See Note 9, above.

[37] Ibid.

[38] World-Nuclear.org, "Thorium," Information Library, Current and Future Generation, updated September 2014, accessed November 21, 2014, http://www.world-nuclear.org/info/Current-and-Future-Generation/Thorium/.

[39] Ibid.

[40] Ambrose Evans-Pritchard, "Obama could kill fossil fuels overnight with a nuclear dash for thorium," the Daily Telegraph, August 29, 2010, http://www.telegraph.co.uk/finance/comment/7970619/Obama-could-kill-fossil-fuels-overnight-with-a-nuclear-dash-for-thorium.html.

[41] World-Nuclear.org, "Thorium," See Note 20, above.

[42] "Thorium-Fuelled Molten Salt Reactors," See Note 9, above.

[43] Ibid.

[44] Ibid.

[45] Wikipedia, s.v. "Thorium-Based Nuclear Power," last modified May 19, 2014, http://en.wikipedia.org/wiki/Thorium-based_nuclear_power#Possible_benefits. See also Richard Martin, Superfuel: Thorium, the Green Energy Source for the Future, New York: Palgrave MacMillan Trade, 2013.

[46] Martin, "Superfuel," 11. See also Robert Hargraves and Ralph Moir, "Liquid Fluoride Nuclear Reactors," American Scientist, July-August 2010.

[47] Ryan Ong, "A boost for nuclear power," China Business Review, May 1, 2010, accessed December 21, 2014, http://www.chinabusinessreview.com/a-boost-for-nuclear-power/.

BS Reporter, "Slowdown not to affect India's nuclear plans," Business Standard, January 21, 2009, accessed December 21, 2014, http://www.business-standard.com/article/economy-policy/slowdown-not-to-affect-india-s-nuclear-plans-109012100091_1.html.

[48] Shalebubble.org, False Promises, Shalebubble.org, Postcarbon Institute, accessed March 29, 2015, http://shalebubble.org/.

[49] Kurt Cobb, "Why Gas Prices Will Soar in the Future," Oilprice.com, May 6, 2013, http://oilprice.com/Energy/Natural-Gas/Why-Natural-Gas-Prices-will-Soar-in-the-Future.html.

[50] "Backgrounder—A Comparison: Land Use by Energy Source—Nuclear, Wind and Solar," Entergy Arkansas, accessed May 23, 2014, http://www.entergy-arkansas.com/content/news/docs/AR_Nuclear_One_Land_Use.pdf.

[51] Ibid.

[52] Edward McMahon, "Walmart Stores Go Small and Urban," Planners Web, February 19, 2014, accessed April 1, 2015, http://plannersweb.com/2014/02/walmart-stores-go-small-urban/.

John Roberts, "Mini-nuclear plants the next frontier of US power supply – or the next Solyndra?"*Executive*, Fox News, July 30, 2013, accessed February 24, 2015, http://www.foxnews.com/politics/2013/07/30/mini-nuclear-plants-next-frontier-us-power-supply-or-next-solyndra/.

[53] Robert I. McDonald, Joseph Fargione, Joe Kiesecker, William M. Miller, and Jimmie Powell, "Energy Sprawl or Energy Efficiency: Climate Policy Impacts on Natural Habitat for the United States of America," PLOS ONE, August 26, 2009, DOI: 10.1371.journal.pone.0006802.

[54] Mark Chew, "Disrupting Coal with Modular Nuclear Reactors," *MIT Entrepreneurship Review*, May 30, 2010, http://miter.mit.edu/articledisrupting-coal-modular-nuclear-reactors/.

Chapter 5

[1] Rob Johnston, "Ten Myths about Nuclear Power," Spiked Magazine, January 9, 2008, http://www.spiked-online.com/newsite/article/4259#.U3O5dfldWSo.

[2] Frontline, "Facts about Radiation," PBS.org, April 1997, http://www.pbs.org/wgbh/pages/frontline/shows/reaction/interact/facts.html.

[3] Ibid.

[4] Mara Hvistendahl, "Coal Ash is More Radioactive than Nuclear Waste," *Scientific American*, December 13, 2007, http://www.scientificamerican.com/article/coal-ash-is-more-radioactive-than-nuclear-waste/.

[5] Nuclear Energy Agency, "The disposal of high-level radioactive waste," *NEA Issue Brief: An analysis of principal nuclear issues*, January 1989, accessed February 2, 2015, http://www.oecd-nea.org/brief/brief-03.html.

World Nuclear Association, "Radioactive Waste Management," world-nuclear.org, updated September 2014, accessed February 2, 2015, http://www.world-nuclear.org/info/Nuclear-Fuel-Cycle/Nuclear-Wastes/Radioactive-Waste-Management/.

[6] "Safely Managing Used Nuclear Fuel," Nuclear Energy Institute, March 2014, http://www.nei.org/Master-Document-Folder/Backgrounders/Fact-Sheets/Safely-Managing-Used-Nuclear-Fuel.

[7] World Nuclear Association, "Processing of Used Nuclear Fuel," world-nuclear.org, updated September 2014, accessed February 2, 2015, http://www.world-nuclear.org/info/Nuclear-Fuel-Cycle/Fuel-Recycling/Processing-of-Used-Nuclear-Fuel/.

[8] Spencer and Loris, "Dispelling Myths," 91, see note 2, above.

[9] "Environment and Health in Electricity Generation," World Nuclear Association, November 2013, http://www.world-nuclear.org/info/Energy-and-Environment/Environment-and-Health-in-Electricity-Generation/.

[10] "Myths and Facts about Nuclear Energy: Synopsis of Common Myths about Nuclear Energy and Corresponding Facts that Refute Them," Nuclear Energy Institute, accessed May 23, 2014, http://www.nei.org/Knowledge-Center/Backgrounders/Fact-Sheets/Myths-Facts-About-Nuclear-Energy-(1).

[11] "Analysis of Nuclear Power Plants Shows Aircraft Crash Would Not Breach Structures Housing Reactor Fuel," Nuclear Energy Institute, December 23, 2002, http://www.nei.org/News-Media/Media-Room/News-Releases/Analysis-of-Nuclear-Power-Plants-Shows-Aircraft-Cr.

[12] "Uranium Enrichment," World Nuclear Association, April 2014, http://www.world-nuclear.org/info/Nuclear-Fuel-Cycle/Conversion-Enrichment-and-Fabrication/Uranium-Enrichment/.

[13] Wikipedia, s.v. "Passive Nuclear Safety," last modified March 21, 2014, http://en.wikipedia.org/wiki/Passive_nuclear_safety.

For more details, see "Safety Related Terms for Advanced Nuclear Plants," IAEA-TECDOC-626, International Atomic Energy Agency, September 1991, http://www-pub.iaea.org/MTCD/publications/PDF/te_626_web.pdf.

[14] Pushker A. Kharecha and James E. Hansen, "Prevented Mortality and Greenhouse Gas Emissions from Historical and Projected Nuclear Power," *Environmental Science and Techonlogy* pp.4889-4895 March 15, 2013, DOI: 10.1021/es3051197 http://pubs.acs.org/doi/abs/10.1021/es3051197.

[15] "Life-Saving Case for Nuclear," World Nuclear News, April 3, 2013, http://www.world-nuclear-news.org/ee_life_saving_case_for_nuclear_0304131.html.

[16] Ibid.

[17] Ibid.

[18] Ibid.

[19] Andrew E. Kramer, "Power for US From Russia's Old Nuclear Weapons?" *The New York Times*, November 9, 2009, http://www.nytimes.com/2009/11/10/business/energy-environment/10nukes.html?_r=0.

"Military Warheads as a Source of Nuclear Fuel," World Nuclear Association, March 2014, http://www.world-nuclear.org/info/nuclear-fuel-cycle/uranium-resources/military-warheads-as-a-source-of-nuclear-fuel/.

[20] "Small Modular Nuclear Reactors," US Department of Energy, accessed May 24, 2014, http://energy.gov/ne/nuclear-reactor-technologies/small-modular-nuclear-reactors.

[21] World Nuclear Association, "Plans For New Reactors Worldwide," *Information Library*, World Nuclear Association, updated March 2013, accessed February 20, 2015, http://www.world-nuclear.org/info/Current-and-Future-Generation/Plans-For-New-Reactors-Worldwide/.

[22] Ibid.

[23] Johnston, "Ten Myths," 90, see note 1, above.

[24] World Nuclear Association, "The Economics of Nuclear Power," *Information Library*, updated June 2015, accessed June 20, 2015, http://www.world-nuclear.org/info/Economic-Aspects/Economics-of-Nuclear-Power/.

[25] Charles R. Frank, Jr., "The Net Benefits of Low- and No-Carbon Electricity Technologies," *Global Economy and Development Working Paper 73*, May, 2014, The Brookings Institution, Washington, DC, http://www.brookings.edu/~/media/research/files/papers/2014/05/19%20low%20carbon%20future%20wind%20solar%20power%20frank/net%20benefits%20final.pdf.

[26] Devindra Hardawar, "Bill Gates: The Good Thing about Nuclear Is Its Lack of Innovation," VentureBeat.com, May 3, 2011, http://venturebeat.com/2011/05/03/bill-gates-nuclear-power/.

[27] Nicolas Cooper, Daisuke Minakata, Miroslav Begovic, and John Crittenden, "Should We Consider Using Liquid Fluoride Thorium Reactors for Power Generation?" *Viewpoint, Environmental Science and Technology*, 2011, 45 (15), 6237-6238, DOI: 10.1021/es2021318.

[28] "Thorium-Fuelled Molten Salt Reactors: Report for the All Party Parliamentary Group on Thorium Energy," The Weinberg Foundation, June 2013, http://www.the-weinberg-foundation.org/wp-content/uploads/2013/06/Thorium-Fuelled-Molten-Salt-Reactors-Weinberg-Foundation.pdf.

[29] TerraPower, "Jumpstarting Advanced Reactors," TerraPower LLC, accessed August 13, 2015, http://terrapower.com/pages/progress.

[30] TerraPower, "Ideas to Change the World," TerraPower LLC, accessed August 13 2015, http://terrapower.com/pages/benefits.

[31] TerraPower, "Environmentally Sound Solution to the Energy Crisis," TerraPower, LLC, accessed August 13, 2015, http://terrapower.com/pages/environment.

[32] TerraPower, "Minimizing Security Risks," TerraPower LLC, accessed August 13, 2015, http://terrapower.com/pages/proliferation-resistance.

[33] TerraPower, "Safely Providing Base Load Power," TerraPower LLC, accessed August 13, 2015, http://terrapower.com/pages/safety.

[34] "Safely Managing Used Nuclear Fuel," 97, see note 13, above.

[35] "Achieving Universal Energy Access," United Nations Foundation, accessed May 22, 2014, http://www.unfoundation.org/what-we-do/issues/energy-and-climate/clean-energy-development.html.

Chapter 6

[1] Daniel Sperling, Deborah Gordon, and Arnold Schwarzenegger, *Two Billion Cars: Driving Toward Sustainability,* New York: Oxford University Press, 2010.

[2] Office of the Press Secretary, "Obama Administration Finalizes Historic 54.5 MPG Fuel Efficiency Standards," The White House, August 28, 2012, http://www.whitehouse.gov/the-press-office/2012/08/28/obama-administration-finalizes-historic-545-mpg-fuel-efficiency-standard.

[3] Kirby Garlitos, "2013 Trident Iceni Grand Tourer," TopSpeed, August 23, 2012, http://www.topspeed.com/cars/others/2013-trident-iceni-grand-tourer-ar134041.html.

[4] Doron Levin, "Toyota Prius Plug-in Drops in Price, Amid Waning Interest," CNN.com, October 15, 2013, http://features.blogs.fortune.cnn.com/2013/10/15/toyota-prius/.

[5] Zifei Yang, "Light-Duty Vehicle Efficiency Standards, EU," The International Council on Clean Transportation, December 2014, accessed May 30, 2015, http://www.theicct.org/sites/default/files/info-tools/pvstds/EU_PVstds-facts_dec2014.pdf.

[6] Peter Mock, *European Vehicle Market Statistics: Pocketbook 2013,* Berlin: The International Council on Clean Transportation, 2013, 41, http://www.theicct.org/sites/default/files/publications/EU_vehiclemarket_pocketbook_2013_Web.pdf.

[7] Brad Tuttle, "Why This Might be the Beginning of the End for the Toyota Prius," *Money,* Time Magazine, Jan 6, 2015, accessed March 15, 2015, http://time.com/money/3654905/toyota-prius-hybrids-sales-decline/.

[8] Russ Rader, "Hybrids cost insurers more than identical vehicles running on gas," *Status Report Vol.43 No.7,* Insurance Institute for Highway Safety Highway Loss Data

Institute, September 9, 2008, accessed May 31, 2015, http://www.iihs.org/iihs/sr/statusreport/article/43/7/2.

[9] NerdWallet, "How Hybrid and Electric Vehicles Affect Your Auto Insurance Quotes," *Vehicle Insurance,* March 31, 2015, NerdWallet, http://www.nerdwallet.com/blog/insurance/2015/03/31/auto-insurance-quotes-hybrid-electric-cars/.

[10] Wheels.ca, "$8,000 hybrid premium buys a lot of gas," Wheels.ca *News and Features,* April 19, 2011, http://www.wheels.ca/8000-hybrid-premium-buys-a-lot-of-gas/.

[11] Don Sherman, "All Hail the Small-Block V8: Gen V Revealed for C7 Corvette," *Car and Driver,* October 2012, http://www.caranddriver.com/news/gen-v-small-block-v-8-specs-and-details-on-the-c7-engine-news.

[12] "How an Electric Car Motor Works," *Cars Direct,* March 14, 2012, http://www.carsdirect.com/green-cars/how-an-electric-car-motor-works.

[13] "Gas Station Statistics," Statisticbrain.com, accessed January 1, 2014, http://statisticbrain.com/gas-station-statistics.

[14] Todd Sperry, "Electric car crashes could pose new risk for first responders, group says," *CNN,* December 28, 2012, accessed January 12, 2016, http://www.cnn.com/2012/12/28/us/electric-car-safety/.

[15] John O'Dell, "Hybrid Sales Soar in November," Edmunds, December 6, 2011, http://www.edmunds.com/industry-center/analysis/hybrid-sales-soar-in-november.html.

[16] Alex Kuhlman, *Peak Oil News,* accessed May 21, 2014, http://www.oildecline.com/news.htm.

[17] Gail Tverburg, "Oil Discoveries Have Been Declining Since 1964," *Our Finite World,* March 2007, http://gailtheactuary.files.wordpress.com/2007/03/oil-discoveries.jpeg.

[18] Kenneth Ameduri, "FutureMoneyTrends.com Forecasts 2012 Energy Oil Shock in New Micro Documentary," *Alaska Dispatch News,* November 23, 2011, accessed January 16, 2016, http://www.adn.com/article/futuremoneytrendscom-forecasts-2012-energy-oil-shock-new-micro-documentary.

[19] Christopher Helman, "The 10 Biggest Oil and Gas Discoveries of 2013," *Forbes Magazine,* January 8, 2014, http://www.forbes.com/sites/christopherhelman/2014/01/08/the-10-biggest-oil-and-gas-discoveries-of-2013/.

[20] "Newt Gingrich Says US May Have 'Three Times as much Oil' as Saudi Arabia," Politifact.com, February 24, 2012, http://www.politifact.com/truth-o-meter/statements/2012/feb/24/newt-gingrich/newt-gingrich-says-us-may-have-three-times-much-oi/.

[21] Institute for Energy Research, "*Encyclopedia Entry*: Oil Shale," Institute for Energy Research, accessed December 6, 2014, http://instituteforenergyresearch.org/topics/encyclopedia/oil-shale/.

[22] Dr. Nafeez Ahmed, "Write-down of two-thirds of US shale oil explodes fracking myth," May 22, 2014, *Environment Earth Insight, The Guardian* http://www.theguardian.com/environment/earth-insight/2014/may/22/two-thirds-write-down-us-shale-oil-gas-explodes-fracking-myth.

[23] Steve Horn, "Drilling Deeper: New Report Casts Doubt on Fracking Production Numbers," October 26, 2010, DeSmogBlog, http://www.desmogblog.com/2014/10/27/drilling-deeper-post-carbon-institute-fracking-production-numbers.

[24] James Hamilton, "Future Production from US Shale or Tight Oil," Econbrowser, December 18, 2012, http://econbrowser.com/archives/2012/12/future_producti.

[25] Troy Hooper, "'Black Sunday': Lessons from Thirty Years Ago Coloring Colorado Oil Shale Debate Today," *The Colorado Independent*, May 2, 2012, http://www.coloradoindependent.com/119367/black-sunday-lessons-from-30-years-ago-coloring-colorado-oil-shale-debate-today.

[26] The Associated Press, "Chevron giving up oil shale lease in Colorado," *the Denver Post*, February 28, 2012, accessed December 14, 2014, http://www.denverpost.com/search/ci_20061466.

[27] Troy Hooper, "Chevron giving up oil shale research in western Colorado to pursue other projects," *The Colorado Independent*, February 29, 2012, accessed January 12, 2016, http://www.coloradoindependent.com/114365/chevron-giving-up-oil-shale-research-in-western-colorado-to-pursue-other-projects.

[28] Kurt Cobb, "Geology beats technology: Shell shuts down oil shale pilot project," *OilVoice Magazine*, Edition 20, November 2013, p.48, http://www.oilvoice.com/magazine/editions/oilvoice_20_November2013.pdf.

[29] National Commission on the BP Deepwater Horizon Oil Spill, "The History of Oil and Offshore Gas in the United States (Long Version), Staff Working Paper Number 22," Encyclopedia of Earth, June 8, 2012, http://www.eoearth.org/files/154601_154700/154673/historyofdrillingstaffpaper22.pdf.

[30] Martina Fuchs, Christopher Johnson, Karen Norton, Joe Brock, and Barbara Lewis, "Factbox—Oil Production Cost Estimates by Country," Reuters, July 28, 2009, http://www.reuters.com/article/2009/07/28/oil-cost-factbox-idUSL512407420090728.

"The Real Reason Gas Costs $4 a Gallon," NPR, April 2, 2012, http://www.npr.org/blogs/money/2012/04/02/149684373/the-real-reason-gas-costs-4-a-gallon.

[31] "World Proven Crude Oil Reserves by Country, 1960–2012," Organization of the Petroleum Exporting Countries, accessed May 20, 2014, http://opec.org/library/ Annual percent20statistical percent20bulletin/interactive/current/FileZ/xl/t31.htm.

[32] Conglin Xu, Laura Bell, "Global reserves, oil production show increases for 2014," *Oil and Gas Journal*, December 1, 2014, accessed May 25, 2015, http://www.ogj.com/ articles/print/volume-112/issue-12/special-report-worldwide-report/global-reserves-oil-production-show-increases-for-2014.html.

[33] Ibid.

[34] Matthew Simmons, *Twilight in the Desert: The Coming Saudi Oil Shock and the World Economy*, Hoboken, NJ: Wiley, 2006.

[35] Praveen Ghanta, "Is Peak Oil Real? A List of Countries Past Peak," The Oil Drum, July 19, 2009, http://www.theoildrum.com/node/5576.

[36] Bill Powers, "The Popping of the Shale Gas Bubble," *Forbes*.com, September 3, 2014, accessed March 29, 2015, http://www.forbes.com/sites/billpowers/2014/09/03/ the-popping-of-the-shale-gas-bubble/.

[37] Wikipedia, s.v. "List of Countries by Population," last modified May 18, 2014, http://en.wikipedia.org/wiki/List_of_countries_by_population.

"Population Figures by Country," One World Nations Online, May 4, 2014, http:// www.nationsonline.org/oneworld/population-by-country.htm.

[38] "World Fuel Ethanol Production," Renewable Fuels Association, accessed January 12, 2016, http://www.ethanolrfa.org/resources/industry/statistics/world/.

[39] Ag Decision Maker, "Iowa Cash Corn and Soybean Prices," File A2-11, Iowa State Extension, May 2014, http://www.extension.iastate.edu/agdm/crops/pdf/a2-11.pdf. Thomas Capehart, "Corn: Background," USDA Economic Research Service, May 14, 2014.

[40] Economic Research Service, "Agriculture in Brazil and Argentina, Executive Summary, WRS-01-3," United States Department of Agriculture, May 30, 2012, http://www.ers.usda.gov/ersDownloadHandler.ashx?file=/media/295599/wrs013b 1_.pdf.

[41] Ibid.

[42] Michael D. Edgerton, "Increasing Crop Productivity to Meet Global Need for Feed, Food, and Fuel," *Plant Physiology*, January 2009, DOI: 10.1104/pp.108.130195, http:// www.ncbi.nlm.nih.gov/pmc/articles/PMC2613695/.

[43] Richard D. Taylor and Won W. Koo, "2011 Outlook of the US and World Corn and Soybean Industries, 2010–2020," Center for Agricultural Policies and Trade Studies, North Dakota State University, July 2011, http://ageconsearch.umn.edu/bitstream/115564/2/AAE682.pdf.

[44] Robert Wisner, "Is China About to Drop Out of the Corn Export Market?" *AgDM Newsletter*, October 2004, http://www.extension.iastate.edu/agdm/articles/wisner/WisOct04.htm.

Patrick Kirchhofer, "Chinese Corn Production," *Interbusiness Issues*, November 2011, http://www.peoriamagazines.com/ibi/2011/nov/chinese-corn-production.

[45] Susanne Retke Schill, "300-Bushel Corn is Coming," *Ethanol Producer Magazine*, October 3, 2007, http://ethanolproducer.com/articles/3330/300-bushel-corn-is-coming.

[46] Vijai Kumar Gupta, Maria G. Tuohy, eds., *Biofuel Technologies: Recent Developments*, Springer-Verlag, Berlin Heidelberg 2013, DOI: 10.1007/978-3-642-34519-7.

[47] Renewable Fuels Association, "Accelerating Industry Innovation: 2012 Ethanol Industry Outlook," *Renewable Fuels Association*, 2011, accessed December 30, 2014, http://ethanolrfa.3cdn.net/d4ad995ffb7ae8fbfe_1vm62ypzd.pdf.

[48] "Industry Resources: Co-products," Renewable Fuels Association, March 2014, http://www.ethanolrfa.org/pages/industry-resources-coproducts.

[49] National Corn Growers' Association, *2011 World of Corn*, Wautoma, WI: Waushara County University of Wisconsin Extension, 2011, http://waushara.uwex.edu/files/2012/03/NCGA-corn-usage-2010.pdf.

Chapter 7

[1] Adam J. Liska, Haishun S. Yang, Virgil R. Bremer, Terry J. Klopfenstein, Daniel T. Walters, Galen E. Erickson, and Kevin G. Cassman, "Improvements in Life Cycle Energy Efficiency and Greenhouse Gas Emissions of Corn Ethanol," *Journal of Industrial Ecology*, 2008, DOI: 10.1111/j.1530-9290.2008.105x.

[2] GrowthEnergy, "Jobs, Environment, and Energy Independence," *Roadmap to a Greener America*, accessed May 31, 2015, http://www.growthenergy.org/images/reports/growth_energy_roadmaptogreeneramerica.pdf.

[3] Gary Z. Whitten, "Air Quality and Ethanol in Gasoline," paper presented at the Ninth Annual National Ethanol Conference, Smog Reyes, February 16–18, 2004, http://www.oregon.gov/energy/renew/biomass/docs/forum/whitten2004.pdf.

[4] Ibid.

[5] "US Cancer Statistics: An Interactive Atlas," Centers for Disease Control and Prevention, accessed May 20, 2014, http://apps.nccd.cdc.gov/DCPC_INCA/DCPC_INCA.aspx.

[6] Daniel O'Brien, Mark Woolverton, and Robert Wisner, "Impact of High Corn Prices on Ethanol Profitability," *Renewable Energy Newsletter,* August 2008, http://www.agmrc.org/renewable_energy/ethanol/impact-of-high-corn-prices-on-ethanol-profitability/.

[7] "The Real Price of Gasoline, Report No. 3: An Analysis of the Hidden External Costs Consumers Pay to Fuel Their Automobiles," International Center for Technology Assessment, November 1998, http://www.ethanol.org/pdf/contentmgmt/The_Real_Price_of_Gas.pdf.

[8] Ibid.

[9] Clean Fuels Development Coalition, *Ethanol Fact Book: A Compilation of Information about Fuel Ethanol,* Washington, DC: Clean Fuels Development Coalition, 2010, http://www.growthenergy.org/images/uploads/CFDC_2010_Ethanol_Fact_Book.pdf.

[10] "How Ethanol is Made," Renewable Fuels Association, accessed May 21, 2014, http://www.ethanolrfa.org/pages/how-ethanol-is-made.

[11] Paul Trupo, "US On Track to Become World's Largest Ethanol Exporter in 2011," *USDA Foreign Agricultural Service,* July 20, 2011, http://apps.fas.usda.gov/info/iatr/072011_Ethanol_IATR.pdf.

[12] Eric Evarts, "EPA Issues Final Approval for Sale of E15 Ethanol Fuel," *Consumer Reports,* June 21, 2012, http://www.consumerreports.org/cro/news/2012/06/epa-issues-final-approval-for-sale-of-e15-ethanol-fuel/index.htm.

[13] US Department of Energy, "Flex-Fuel Vehicles," Fuel Economy.gov, May 19, 2014, http://www.fueleconomy.gov/feg/flextech.shtml.

[14] Todd Neeley, "Poet to Spread the Cellulosic Ethanol Wealth," *Ethanol Blog,* DTN, April 30, 2010, http://www.dtnprogressivefarmer.com/dtnag/view/blog/getBlog.do;jsessionid=2A3539063E5D52237D50F665A3860AA4.agfreejvm1?blogHandle=ethanol&blogEntryId=8a82c0bc2803bb3c01284f86808f03ca.

[15] "History: Race and All-Time Stats," Indianapolis Motor Speedway, accessed May 25, 2014, http://www.indianapolismotorspeedway.com/indy500/history/stats/.

[16] Cindy Zimmerman, "NASCAR Hits Three Million Miles on E15," Domestic Fuel, October 10, 2012, http://domesticfuel.com/2012/10/10/nascar-hits-three-million-miles-on-e15/.

[17] Energy Information Administration, "U.S. ethanol exports in 2014 reach highest level since 2011," *Today in Energy*, March 26, 2015, accessed July 1, 2015, http://www.eia.gov/todayinenergy/detail.cfm?id=20532.

[18] Holly Jessen, "US Ethanol, DDGS Exports Break Records in 2010," *Ethanol Producer Magazine*, February 15, 2011, http://www.ethanolproducer.com/articles/7508/u-s-ethanol-ddgs-exports-break-records-in-2010.

[19] "Commodity Products: Trading Corn for the Ethanol Crush," AC-406/100/0410, CME Group, accessed May 25, 2014, http://www.cmegroup.com/trading/agricultural/files/AC-406_DDG_CornCrush_042010.pdf.

[20] Cole Gustafson, "Biofuels Economics: How Many Acres Will Be Needed for Biofuels? Part I" North Dakota State University, June 26, 2008, http://www.ag.ndsu.edu/news/columns/biofuels-economics/biofuels-economics-how-many-acres-will-be-needed-for-biofuels-part-i/; and "Part 2," July 10, 2008, http://www.ag.ndsu.edu/news/columns/biofuels-economics/biofuel-economics-how-many-acres-will-be-needed-for-biofuels-part-ii/.

[21] "Policy Update 6: US EPA Renewable Fuel Standard 2: Final Rule Summary," International Council on Clean Transportation, April 2, 2010, http://theicct.org/sites/default/files/publications/policyupdate6_rfs2.pdf.

[22] Raya Widenoja, "How Will the U.S. Produce 36 Billion Gallons of Biofuel by 2022?" Worldwatch Institute, accessed May 30, 2015, http://www.worldwatch.org/node/5600.

Chapter 8

[1] Hosein Shapouri, Paul W. Gallagher, Ward Nefstead, Rosalie Schwartz, Stacey Noe, and Roger Conway, "2008 Energy Balance for the Corn-Ethanol Industry," USDA Agricultural Economic Report Number 846, June 2010, http://www.usda.gov/oce/reports/energy/2008Ethanol_June_final.pdf.

[2] Adam J. Liska, Haishun S. Yang, Virgil R. Bremer, Terry J. Klopfenstein, Daniel T. Walters, Galen E. Erickson, and Kevin G. Cassman, "Improvements in Life Cycle Energy Efficiency and Greenhouse Gas Emissions of Corn Ethanol," *Journal of Industrial Ecology*, 2008, DOI: 10.1111/j.1530-9290.2008.105x.

Don Hofstrand, "Efficiency and environmental improvements of corn ethanol production," AgMRC Renewable Energy Newsletter, July 2009, accessed My 31, 2015, http://www.agmrc.org/renewable_energy/ethanol/efficiency-and-environmental-improvements-of-corn-ethanol-production/.

[3] Renewable Fuels Association, "Building Bridges to a More Sustainable Future: 2011 Ethanol Industry Outlook," p.22, Renewable Fuels Association, 2010, accessed December 30, 2014, http://www.ethanolrfa.org/page/-/2011%20RFA%20 Ethanol%20Industry%20Outlook.pdf?nocdn=1.

[4] Renewable Fuels Association, "Ethanol Facts: Environment," updated March 2014, accessed December 29, 2014, http://www.ethanolrfa.org/pages/ ethanol-facts-environment.

[5] American Cancer Society, "Benzene," *Learn About Cancer—Other Carcinogens, In the Workplace,* last revised December 9, 2013, accessed March 25, 2015 http://www. cancer.org/cancer/cancercauses/othercarcinogens/intheworkplace/benzene.

[6] GolfInfoGuide.com, "By the Numbers: USA Golfers and Golf Courses," GolfInfoGuide.com (2012 figures) accessed July 7, 2015, http://golf-info-guide.com/ golf-tips/golf-in-the-usa/by-the-numbers-usa-golfers-and-golf-courses/.

[7] Robert White, Ron Lamberty, "PEI Report Shows Actual Cost of Installing E15 is Much Lower than Claimed by Ethanol Opponents," *Renewable Fuels Association,* September 10, 2013, accessed May 31, 2015, http://www.ethanolrfa.org/news/entry/ pei-report-shows-actual-cost-of-installing-e15-is-much-lower-than-claimed/.

[8] Eyal Aronoff and Nathan Taft, "Is the Gasoline Gallon Equivalent an Accurate Measure of Mileage for Ethanol and Methanol Fuel Blends?" *Fuel Freedom Foundation,* August 2013, accessed May 31, 2015, http://www.fuelfreedom.org/wp-content/ uploads/white-paper_GGE-Sept-2013.pdf.

Institute for Energy Resourcefulness, "3. Value of Ethanol in Current and Near-Future US Vehicles," *The Potential of Ethanol,* accessed May 31, 2015, http://www. energyresourcefulness.org/Fuels/ethanol_fuels/value_of_ethanol_in_current_ and_near_future_vehicles.html.

[9] Rex Weber, "Ethanol-Blended Fuels," *National Renewable Energy Laboratory,* accessed May 31, 2015, http://www.nrel.gov/education/pdfs/educational_resources/high_ school/teachers_guide_ethanol.pdf.

[10] Ibid.

R.L. Nielsen, "Corn Grain Yield Trends: Eyes of the Beholder," *Corny News Network,* Purdue University, Indiana, June 15, 2006, accessed May 31, 2015, http://www.agry. purdue.edu/ext/corn/news/articles.06/YieldTrends-0615.html.

[11] Peter Thomison, Alexander Linsey, Allen Geyer, and Rich Minyo, "Drought-Tolerant Corn Hybrids," *Crop Observation and Recommendation Network (CORN) Newsletter,*

July 2013, http://corn.osu.edu/newsletters/2013/c.o.r.n.-newsletter-2013-07/drought-tolerant-corn-hybrids.

[12] William Pentland, "The Coming Food Crisis: Blame Ethanol?" *Forbes*, July 28, 2012, accessed May 31, 2015, http://www.forbes.com/sites/williampentland/2012/07/28/the-coming-food-crisis-blame-ethanol/.

[13] Taxpayers for Common Sense, "Updated: Taxpayer Supports for Corn Ethanol in Federal Legislation," *Fact Sheets*, Taxpayers for Common Sense, April 15, 2014, accessed May 31, 2015, http://www.taxpayer.net/library/article/updated-taxpayer-supports-for-corn-ethanol-in-federal-legislation.

Chapter 9

[1] Bill Canis, "Battery Manufacturing for Hybrid and Electric Vehicles: Policy Issues," Congressional Research Service, April 4, 2013, accessed May 31, 2015, https://www.fas.org/sgp/crs/misc/R41709.pdf.

[2] Adam J. Liska, Haishun S. Yang, Virgil R. Bremer, Terry J. Klopfenstein, Daniel T. Walters, Galen E. Erickson, and Kevin G. Cassman, "Improvements in Life Cycle Energy Efficiency and Greenhouse Gas Emissions of Corn Ethanol," *Journal of Industrial Ecology*, 2008, DOI: 10.1111/j.1530-9290.2008.105x.

Conclusion

[1] "Achieving Universal Energy Access," United Nations Foundation, accessed May 23, 2014 http://www.unfoundation.org/what-we-do/issues/energy-and-climate/clean-energy-development.html.